CREDIT SECRETS

3 BOOKS IN 1
WITH AN UNPUBLISHED WORK

The Complete Guide To Finding Out All the Secrets To Fix Your Credit Report and Boost Your Score. Learn How To Improve Your Finances and Have a Wealthy Lifestyle.

DAVE ROBERT WARREN GRAHAM

©Copyright 2020 by Dave Robert Warren Graham

- All rights reserved –

Wealth Management Academy IPH

ISBN Paperback: 9781801117975
ISBN Hardcover: 9781801117968

The content contained within this book may not be reproduced, duplicated or transmitted without direct written permission from the author or the publisher.

Under no circumstances will any blame or legal responsibility be held against the publisher, or author, for any damages, reparation, or monetary loss due to the information contained within this book. Either directly or indirectly.

Legal Notice:
This book is copyright protected. This book is only for personal use. You cannot amend, distribute, sell, use, quote or paraphrase any part, or the content within this book, without the consent of the author or publisher.

Disclaimer Notice:
Please note the information contained within this document is for educational and entertainment purposes only. All effort has been executed to present accurate, up to date, and reliable, complete information. No warranties of any kind are declared or implied. Readers acknowledge that the author is not engaging in the rendering of legal, financial, medical or professional advice. The content within this book has been derived from various sources. Please consult a licensed professional before attempting any techniques outlined in this book.
By reading this document, the reader agrees that under no circumstances is the author responsible for any losses, direct or indirect, which are incurred as a result of the use of the information contained within this document, including, but not limited to, — errors, omissions, or inaccuracies

This book is dedicated to those who, like me a few years ago, want to improve their financial future.

To my best friend Nans. Thanks to him for his valuable advice made me a successful entrepreneur and investor.

…and now that I live the life I want with my family and help my loved ones, I am very excited to share what I know with you

Dave R. W. Graham

Book 1:
Credit Score Secrets

The Proven Guide To Increase Your Credit Score Once And For All. Manage Your Money, Your Personal Finance, And Your Debt To Achieve Financial Freedom Effortlessly.

◆◆◆◆

Book 2:
Credit Repair Secrets

Learn the Strategies and Techniques of Consultants and Credit Attorneys to Fix your Bad Debt and Improve your Business or Personal Finance. Including Dispute Letters.

◆◆◆◆

Book 3:
The Best Credit Habits
(*Unpublished Work*)

Find Out in Simple Steps How To Manage Your Credit and Get A Happier Financial Life.

◆◆◆◆

Table Of Contents

BOOK 1:
CREDIT SCORE SECRETS 1

Introduction 3
Chapter 1. How to Get Started 9
Chapter 2. Understanding Credit Score 17
Chapter 3. How to Manage your Credit Cards 25
Chapter 4. Ways to Make and Save More Money with a High Credit Score 33
Chapter 5. Tips and Tricks to Raise Your Credit Score and Get 730+ Point 43
Chapter 6. Most Common Errors Found in Credit Reports and How to Avoid Them 51
Chapter 7. Managing Debt 55
Chapter 8. Identity Theft 61
Chapter 9. How Credit System Works 69
Chapter 10. Credit Scoring Myth 79
Chapter 11. Credit Bureau and Credit Errors 85
Chapter 12. How Fast and How Many Points Will a Credit Score Improve 91
Chapter 13. Techniques to Rebuild your Credit 97
Chapter 14. Resolving Bad Credit Situation 101
Conclusion 107

BOOK 2:
CREDIT REPAIR SECRETS 111

Introduction 113
Chapter 1. How to Get Started 119

Chapter 2. Understanding FCRA and Section 609 127
Chapter 3. How to Remove Hard Inquiries from Your Credit Report 135
Chapter 4. What the Credit Bureaus and the Lawyers Do Not Want You to Know 143
Chapter 5. Advice Nobody Tell You... 147
Chapter 6. Your Financial Freedom 153
Chapter 7. Little Known Facts About Credit.................................. 161
Chapter 8. Effective Strategies for Repairing your Credit................ 165
Chapter 9. Controlling Various Kinds of Debt 173
Chapter 10. Guaranteed Methods to Protect Credit Score 181
Chapter 11. The Credit Bureau 185
Chapter 12. How to Overcome Credit Card Debt.......................... 190
Chapter 13. Credit Repair from Scratch 197
Conclusion... 203
BONUS:
The Best Templates You Can Use to Work with Section 609 207

BOOK 3:
THE BEST CREDIT HABITS (UNPUBLISHED WORK) 217

Introduction 219
Chapter 1. How to Get Started To Build Your Credit 221
Chapter 2. Budgeting And Saving... 227
Chapter 3. The Importance of Investing 231
Chapter 4. How To Ensure Customers Fall In love With Your Business 237
Chapter 5. What Is Credit Counseling?.. 243
Chapter 6. Right Mindset for Credit Management......................... 248
Conclusion... 252

AUTHOR'S NOTE 256

BOOK 1: CREDIT SCORE SECRETS

The Proven Guide To Increase Your Credit Score Once And For All. Manage Your Money, Your Personal Finance, And Your Debt To Achieve Financial Freedom Effortlessly

Introduction

In its simplest terms, a credit score is a number that represents your financial standing and is used by lenders (credit card companies, mortgage companies, auto loan companies, etc.). This number is determined by your current debt, your payment history, and your ability to pay off any debt in which you are trying to gain. There are many other factors that define a credit score, but this is the simplest way to explain it. An easy way to see how your credit score is shaped, is by looking at the 4 main things they look at:

1. Who do you owe money to?
2. How much do you owe?
3. How much you have already paid?
4. How efficient you are in paying what you owe (This is by far, the most important one)

One thing to note: There are multiple credit scoring models out there. What I have noticed is that most credit card companies tend to use a specific scoring model that affects certain loans, such as credit cards.

Failure is an experience that no one would like to go through. However, with a good plan and guidance, you will be able to overcome it.

If there are accounts or cards whose balance you have successfully paid out, do not close them. It is always good to view the clean criminal record. This phase has a triple advantage. First, it seems they have paid their debts. Secondly, it shows your expertise in paying more types of credit and thirdly, it shows a more extended credit history.

This may not be explicitly mentioned anywhere, but it is just common sense. Increasing assets increases reliability. If you have sufficient resources, you will be able to mortgage them for credit. So, creditors will give you credit for getting a good guarantee in exchange for their risk. Avoid construction liabilities like credit card bills as it will affect your negative rating.

Always keep in touch with them and express your inability to pay, if that is the case, and see if it is possible to make an agreement in any way. After all, they want their money and not the rating to fall.

10 Fundamental Reasons to Have Good Credit

1. Get funds to start or grow your business.
2. You will have access to money for emergencies.
3. You can qualify to buy a home and build equity.
4. Borrow unsecured money for college.
5. Access to reward programs that offer free travel.
6. Zero or low interest auto loans.
7. No deposits on utilities and some leases.
8. Qualify for job opportunities that require decent credit and save thousands on insurance policies each year.
9. Purchase protection from merchants.

10. Travel protection and zero liability rental car insurance.

How to Improve Your Personal Finance: Managing Your Bad and Good Debt to Raise Your Incomes?

It's possible to improve your credit score. Your score is calculated using many different factors that carry different weights. The following is just some general advice on improving your score before we get into the specifics.

The best thing that you can do to get your credit score up is to make payments on time. As soon as you start missing payments, your score will plummet. A delinquency can turn into a negative item that is much harder to remove. If you do miss payments, communicating and maintaining a good relationship with your creditor is critical. Having a broad mix of credit types on your report also helps to improve your score. Having five credit cards, for examples, does not look as good as having two cards, an auto loan, a mortgage and a student loan.

How Anyone Can Quickly Raise Their Credit Score

There are steps you can take to start increasing your credit rating.

Get a Copy of Your Credit Reports

Before you can Work out how to boost your credit rating, you need to understand what score you are starting from. The first area you must go to boost your credit score is the credit report because of your credit rating based on the data in your credit file. A credit report is a listing of your repayment history, credit administration, and debt. It might also contain information regarding your accounts, which have gone into some other repossessions or bankruptcies and collections. Order copies of your credit reports from each of the three credit agencies to identify.

Dispute Credit Report Errors

Under the Fair Credit Reporting Act, you have the right. This right permits you to dispute credit report mistakes by writing to the credit agency, which has to investigate the dispute. Entrance snafus by lenders, identity theft, birthdays, or speeches, or readily interchangeable Social Security numbers, can hurt your credit rating. For Instance, if you possess a record of late payments reported since payments represent 35 % of your credit rating, payment on the record of somebody might have an immediate and dramatic effect on your score. The more quickly you get and dispute errors resolved, the sooner you can begin to raise your credit rating.

Prevent New Credit Card Purchases

New credit card purchases will increase your credit use rate--a %age of your credit card accounts to their credit limitations, which make 30 % of your credit rating up. You can calculate it. The higher your accounts are, the greater your credit use will be, and the higher your credit score might be influenced. It is better to maintain your credit use rate. In other words, you need to keep a balance of no more than $3,000 with a limit of 10,000 on a

Credit card. Rather than placing them to decrease the influence to fulfil that goal, pay money for purchases. Prevent the purchase.

Pay off Past-Due Balances

Your payment history makes up 35 % of your credit rating, making it the most crucial determinant of your credit score. The further behind you are in your payments, the more it hurts your credit rating. As soon as you have curbed credit card spending, use the savings to have caught up in your credit card payments until they are billed (the grantor shut off the accounts to future usage) or delivered to a collections service.

Do your best to cover outstanding accounts in total; the bank will then upgrade the account status to "paid in full" that will reveal more favorably on your credit compared to unpaid accounts. Moreover, by continued to take a balance as you pay off an account over the years, you will be subjected to finance fees that are continuing.

Be Patient and Persistent

Patience is used to compute your credit rating, but it is something you have to have while you are fixing your credit score. So, don't expect it to increase in that period your Credit was not ruined immediately. Continue monitoring your Credit, maintaining your spending in check, and paying for your debts on time every month, and over time, you will find a boost on your credit rating.

Pay off Debt

The amount of debt, which you are carrying as a %age of your credit, represents 30 % of your credit rating, which means you are going to need to begin paying down that debt. If you have a positive cash flow, then meaning you get more than you do owe, think about two procedures for paying

Why Do You Have to Manage your Credit Score?

Credit scores are essential tools that help you get approved for different loans such as a car loan, mortgage, or credit cards. They show lenders if you can pay your loan payments on time. Additionally, it helps them decide the rates and terms for your loan, considering the associated risks.

With a good credit score, you could potentially save thousands and rent that apartment, or buy that house or car that you wanted, for less. Your credit scores aren't stored with your credit history (though the history of those loans and repayments stay on your report). These scores come up within a specific range every time a lender request for it.

Credit scores are therefore essential but aren't the only determinant for the rates and terms of your loan. Your credit history, on time repayments, the total debt you accumulated over time, utility bill payments and more are considered before you are given a loan.

Chapter 1.

How to Get Started

Introducing Credit Score

Your credit score has an impact on credit applications in the future, so you want to get it as high as possible. A credit rating of good is the minimum you want to aim for if you want to be approved for credit and get advantageous interest rates quickly. FICO and Vantage Score both indicate that about two-thirds of Americans have a rating of good or better. This statistic shows promise for people who are attempting to build credit. It is not that difficult to do if you are careful with how you use your available credit.

An important aspect for some people is a minimum credit score. Technically, the minimum credit scores a person can have is 300. You may often hear groups talking about a minimum credit score if you want to apply for an account or loan. The truth is that there's no such thing. You do not need to have a minimum credit score to apply for credit.

Mortgage providers (the companies providing credit for home loans) indicate that even people with low credit scores can apply for home loans. The most significant difference is that you may not get favorable terms and reasonable interest rates if your credit score is poor. Many lending institutions require a minimum down payment of 10% and additional security if your credit score is below 580. In contrast, a credit score higher than 580 only necessitates a 3.5% down payment. This example clearly shows why a good credit score is better for people.

How Many Types of Credit Scores Are There?

Businesses have credit scores just like individuals, but the ratings work in a slightly different manner. You may be operating a business and need to take out a loan or purchase a vehicle on finance for company purposes. It is essential to understand the differences between good credit scores for business and that of individuals.

The most significant difference lies in the actual credit scores: business credit scores fall within a range of zero to 100. Similar rules still apply and the closer your business is to a score of 100, the better it will be for your credit applications.

The Experian score is broken down into more segments: high-risk businesses score 1 to 10; medium to high-risk score 11 – 25; medium risk is obtained by businesses with a score of 26 to 50. The segments then become slightly more substantial. Businesses scoring between 51 and 75 pose a low to medium risk for lenders, and the lowest risk is when a business has a score of 76 to 100.

Equifax works slightly differently. They have one rating system for payment history and another for the likelihood that your business will fail. Instead of describing the scores in terms of risk, Equifax gives a ranking based on how you pay or how late your payment is to your creditors. Paying your creditors as agreed gives a score of 90 – 100; if you pay in the 30 days following the due date then your score is 80 – 89. A score of 60 – 79 is attributed for payment 31 to 60 days after the due date. Paying creditors 61 to 90 days late will result in a 40 – 59 credit score; while a score of 20 – 39 is given for payment between days 91 and 120.

The non-FICO scores are called FAKO scores by some consumers. Experian has a credit score for educational use only (Plus Score) between 330 and 830, and Experian Scorex PLUS score is between 300 and 900. Equifax has the Equifax Credit Score between 280 and 850.

Some lenders use an Application Score between 100 and 990, and Credit Optics Score by ID Analytics Inc. between 1 and 999.

Several websites (Trans Union, Equifax, Credit Karma, Credit Sesame etc.) offer different credit scores to consumers but are not used by lenders. Innovis, ChexSystems and PRBC are other companies that produce credit scores used by some lenders.

Here's really all you need to know. You have a Vantage Score from each of the bureaus. They use the exact same formula because they all joined forces to create the formula. You would have the exact same Vantage Score from each bureau if you had the same information in each bureau. Although it's highly unlikely you have the same information in all the bureaus. The Vantage Score is used by only 10% of lenders.

You also a FICO score from each bureau. Used by 90% of credit lenders. This score would also be the same for each bureau if you had the same information in each bureau. This again is highly unlikely.

You also have Industry Specific FICO Scores from each of the bureaus. Credit Cards, Auto Industry, Installment Loan, Personal Finance and finally Mortgage.

Three Major Credit Bureaus, Three Credit Scores, Two Models Rating Agencies

There are 3 main Credit Bureaus that crunch the numbers and create a credit score that defines your score: Trans Union, Equifax, and Experian (There are in fact other companies, smaller ones, but these are the 3 we will focus on). Each Credit Bureau looks at different aspects of your financial profile. What this means is that, for example, Experian will take a heavy consideration on late credit card payments, but Equifax may not focus so much on that

FICO vs. Vantage Scores

FICO Ratings

The ratings given by FICO are shown below along with the corresponding scores.

Fico Score	Rating	What the Score Means
300 – 579	Very poor	• Well below average • For a lender, you are a risky borrower
580 – 669	Fair	• Below average • Many lenders will approve loans

670 – 739	Good	• Near or slightly above average • Most lenders consider this a good score
740 – 799	Very Good	• Above average • You're a dependable borrower
800 – 850	Exceptional	• Well above average • You're an exceptional borrower

People with a credit score between 300 and 579 are said to have a very poor score; this does not mean that the person is financially poor. It is unlikely that these people will be approved for credit. If an application does succeed, then the applicant may need to pay a deposit or additional fee as security.

It is possible to improve this score through proper credit control and gain a better record. People with a good (670 – 739) credit score can easily obtain credit. Additionally, there is a very small chance for these individuals to start making poor credit decisions suddenly.

Most people want to be placed in the category of very good (740 – 799) or have a score of more than 800 to achieve the rating of exceptional. These individuals will be offered the best credit card deals from top lending companies. Another advantage of a high credit score is that you will be given low interest rates when borrowing money.

Vantage Score Ratings

The Vantage Score ratings are slightly different as seen in the following table.

Vantage Score	Rating	What the Score Means
300 – 499	Very poor	• It will be difficult to get credit
500 – 600	Poor	• Some institutions will approve small amounts of credit with high interest rates
601 – 660	Fair	• Some institutions will approve credit more easily but with high interest rates
661 – 780	Good	• You will get credit more easily with competitive interest rates
781 – 850	Excellent	• You will get credit with favorable interest rates from some of the top lending companies

Vantage Score has an evener distribution of scores across the range. Those with very poor scores (300 – 499) have almost no chance of being approved for credit. These people will find it difficult to get credit and struggle to improve the score.

People with a poor (500 – 600) score might get a small amount of credit from some institutions. However, the interest rates will not be good, and some places may ask for security or large deposits to ensure that the company receives their money back. A better position would be a fair score of 601 to 660. Individuals with this rating will get credit more easily but still have some issues with interest rates being high.

A good credit score (661 – 780) will ensure that a person is approved for credit and receive competitive interest rates. Vantage Score considers anything above 700 to be a great score and that number falls within a good rating. The best rating is excellent with scores between 781 and 850. These individuals will receive favorable interest rates and easily be approved for credit from some of the top lending companies.

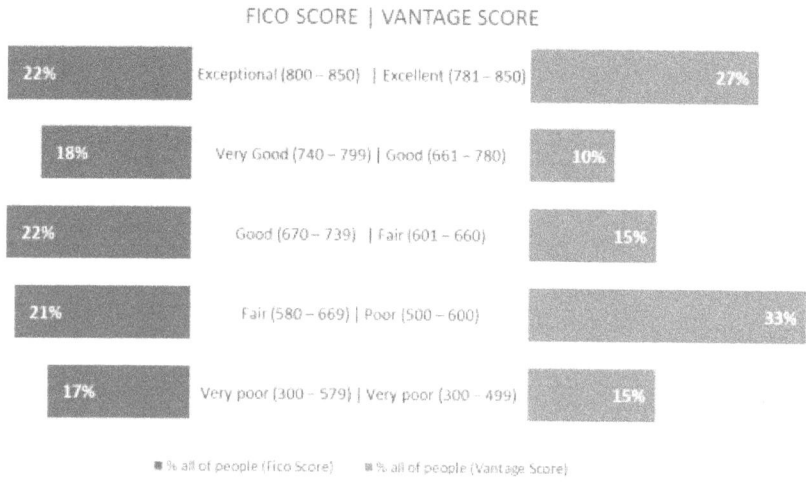

Chapter 2.

Understanding Credit Score

What is a FICO Score?

The credit score structure was formulated by the Fair Isaac Corporation also referred to as FICO. This credit score is utilized by financial institutions. There is other credit score models; however, the FICO score is the one that is most commonly used. Consumers can get and keep high credit scores by simply making sure their debt level remains low, and they maintain an extended history of paying their bills as and when they are due.

In the FICO scoring formula, not all credit reports are scored equally.

Credit scores are weighted based on the particular "score card" that a person falls under.

For example, if the person has filed for bankruptcy, they may be scored using a special "bankruptcy" scorecard.

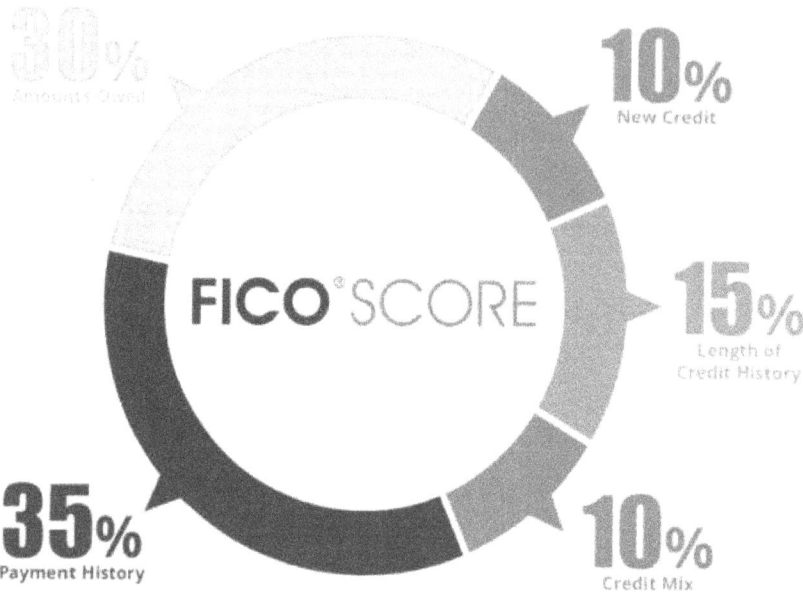

The credit score for a person under one scorecard may be affected differently by s negative event, like a late payment, then of someone with the same event on a different scorecard.

The score card you're on is determined by the most recent significant event in your credit history.

The first 10 scorecards go something like this...

Scorecards 1-5:

1. Those with public records, including judgements and bankruptcy, on their credit report

2. For those with serious delinquencies other than bankruptcies (60, 90, 120 latest, collections, judgments, charge-offs repossessions, etc.).

3. Those with only 1 credit account (very thin files)

4. Those with only 2 credit accounts (thin files)

5. Those with 3 credit accounts only.

Scorecards 6-10 should NOT have ANY grave felonies (the definition of "serious" is unknown)

6. 0-2 years oldest account
7. 2-5 years oldest account
8. 5-12 years oldest account
9. 12-19 years oldest account
10. 19+ years oldest account

There is a total of 12 score cards, and they are subject to change as FICO (formerly Fair Isaac Corp) updates their scoring formula.

How Do You Check Your Credit Score?

It's a common misconception that you will automatically get your credit score when you get a copy of your credit report. This is not entirely the case. Credit reports usually do not include your credit score. It's also important to note that you do not have only one credit score. You will have at least three and more if you include the Vantage Score. They should similar in range but will not usually be the same number because they are an estimate based on a series of calculations.

There are a few different ways you can try to access your credit scores. Look to our list for suggestions:

1. Check with your financial institutions. Many loaners such as credit card companies show your credit score as part of your account for free. If your creditors do not offer this, then you might be able to find the information on your online banking. Wells Fargo, for example, updates your credit score online once a month and shows how the number has changed, and what is most influencing the score. It's as easy as logging in to your account and browsing the offered resources.

2. Just like you can order credit reports, you can also order a copy of your score from the three main credit bureaus, and FICO directly. This is a good option if your banking institution does not offer information or you are doing your yearly credit report check.

3. Some people choose to use credit score services, or free credit monitoring services to keep track of their credit score. Others offer greater resources and protection that charge, but there are many free ones. These are good options for those who are looking to keep track of their credit but don't want to spend the extra money for monitoring or to order directly from FICO.

What Information is in a Credit Report?

Every credit bureau collects a lot of information about you, and all of that is included in your credit report. If someone wants to know about your credit usage in all these years, then one look at the credit report would reveal everything. The report has everything starting from whether you have cleared all your bills on time to the amount of debt that you might owe. The three credit bureaus, that is, Equifax, Experian, and Trans-union, are the ones that collect that information and compile them in the form of a report. All the information included in your report is collected from different sources (that is, lenders).

Whenever you want to apply for any type of loan or credit like student loans, credit cards, mortgage loans, and auto loans, every lender would want to have a look at your credit report. They will be granting you the credit only after they have evaluated your credit report, and everything seems fine. Your stats should match the terms set by them and if not, then you will not be getting your favorable rates.

The information that is present in your credit report is utilized in finding out your credit score. And all that information will be used by lenders to predict what your future behavior with respect to credit is going to be.

Personal Information

This is the list of information that can be used in the future to identify you as a person. All of this information is not utilized to find your credit score. Some of the things that are included in this segment are your name, any misspellings that have been brought to light by creditors, aliases (if any), home addresses (past and current), Social Security Number, employers (past and current) and phone numbers.

Public Records

But any non- financial information or misdemeanors or arrests are not included here. It is solely meant for financial, legal actions, and if you have any public record in your credit report, then that is considered to be bad and you are probably not going to receive credits or loans.

Accounts

There are three categories to these accounts – closed, negative, and open. When you have been on good terms with the creditor, they will report the same. Your accounts will be in a good position. But sometimes you might not find certain account information because it was not reported by the creditors.

Some of the negative things that can be included are bankruptcies, late payments, or any type of account that has been forwarded to the collection or may be charged off. If an account has been transferred or settled, then that might not have any bad impact on your score or report. It would definitely be something that any creditor would look more closely at.

Credit Inquiries

Usually, your credit report might have an inquiry up till two years from when it was made. Some things that are not mentioned in your credit report are your marital information, your education level, or even your bank balance. If a creditor has reported the name of your spouse, then that might be included in a report. But if you have had a divorce and you do not want the name of your spouse on the credit report, then you can proceed with disputing the information displayed on your credit report.

What is a Good Credit Score? How Can I Improve My Credit Rating and Credit Score?

Your credit score is split into several levels, but generally ranges from 300 to 850. The different credit rating levels are label as follows:

- 300 to 600: Bad Credit
- 600 to 649: Poor Credit
- 650 to 699: Fair Credit
- 700 to 749: Good Credit
- 750 + 850: Excellent Credit

The higher your credit score, the better. Better scores allow you to get credit easier, and with lower interest rates. Even when not getting credit, such as when you are renting an apartment, having a better credit rating builds trust with potential landlords.

The best thing that you can do to get your credit score up is to make payments on time. As soon as you start missing payments, your score will plummet. A delinquency can turn into a negative item that is much harder to remove. If you do miss payments, communicating and maintaining a good relationship with your creditor is key.

Chapter 3.

How to Manage your Credit Cards

How to Find Credit Cards with Guaranteed Approval?

What does true mean by promised approval? All credit cards come with some form of basic requirements before you are issued by a business. A key factor in those so-called secured credit cards is that the qualification requirements are usually minimal.

Milestone Master card – Less Than Perfect Credit Considered
The Milestone MasterCard provides a fast and easy application process and the use of all types of credit is encouraged. The card does not require a security deposit and is very welcoming to vulnerable creditors. The Milestone Card may be used anywhere Visa is approved, according to the credit available.

Total Visa Card
The Full Visa Card is another card that does not need a security deposit and provides all the perks of a Visa full-service card. The card allows borrowers

to have a current checking account, and a one-time service fee is charged. The lines of credit available are based on your actual credit score and credit worthiness.

How to Use a Credit Card Responsibly?

Try not to use more than 30% of your credit card's limit

- Make sure to always make payments on time. Even if it is the minimum payment!
- If you have the means, do your best to try and pay off your credit card balance in full each statement (this is not really all that realistic, I certainly couldn't do this in the past. But if you can, do so!)

How to Find Right Credit Card for You?

There is no one size fits all credit card. Depending on your age and profession you will find certain credit cards more advantageous for your specific needs.

Credit cards to get a Balance transfer

Even as credit cards include the capacity accounts, stability switches. Credit card is one, which provides a low fee. If you happen to keep money, there is a stability switch a great way to go. The reduction in the promotional cost (and more the promotional span), the larger the appealing card is. You may require a credit rating that is genuine to qualify.

Subprime credit rating cards

Credit rating cards are among the credit rating card solutions. Those credit rating cards have been aimed, and such cards have expenses and hobby prices. As acceptance is short for people who have a credit rating that is awful, the terms are hard.

Student credit cards

Student Credit Rating cards are those specifically made that those teens have credit rating documents. Student credit rating cards may come, such as a cost or wages on balance transfers. College students commonly must be registered at a licensed 4-year university to become approved to get a student loan scorecard.

Restricted cause cards

Utilize motive Credit cards that are restricted can handiest at locations. Rationale cards function using a fee and fund cost as credit rating cards. Gas credit rating cards and store credit rating cards are cases of motive credit scorecards that are restricted.

Secured credit rating cards

Secured credit cards are an alternative rating repute. Cards call for a protection deposit to be set on the card. It might be additional in some instances -- combined with a default, although the credit rating limitation on a credit rating card is equal to the amount of the deposit left on the card. It is worth noting that you predicted to create payments on your credit card balance.

How to Get an Instalment Loan While Still in Bankruptcy

If you just filed for bankruptcy last week, you will have a very tough time quickly re-establishing credit. If some time has passed, you have a good shot at getting started though. It may be that a little more waiting is required before you can qualify for new credit lines. Even a relatively small mistake like maxing out a credit card or missing a utility bill can harm your credit score. Some might try to repair their credit from transactions they didn't think would harm their credit like closing an old account or even applying for a new loan. Then there might some who are trying to repair their credit after a major transgression like the declaration of bankruptcy. According to the reasons that have harmed your credit score, the time taken for repair will differ. This isn't a precise estimate and is only used as examples for your understanding. The recovery period will depend on several factors, along with the existing information on your credit report. If you have a long-standing credit history of timely payments, it is easier to repair any damage. If your credit history is riddled with defaulting on payments, then it will take longer to fix any damage. Apart from this, your existing score matters too. Applicants that have either no credit or bad credit scores are seen to be high-risk borrowers, and that results in them having a decreased chance of being approved for a credit card or loan. Conversely, individuals with good credit scores are seen to be low-risk borrowers, and this increases the likelihood of them getting their applications approved. Credit scores by themselves do not control whether your loan request is approved or not. They are simply numbers created from a credit report. Lenders use them as a tool. Standards are set for what credit scores are acceptable, and the final decision is made.

It does take a bit of time, but if you develop your credit well, that can make your credit scores improve and increase your chances of getting approval.

How to Get Lender to Remove a Lot Days Late?

If you are currently behind on payments, ask the creditor if you can negotiate for a lower settlement amount, which includes their removing the late payments from your credit record after you have settled your debt. If they still want the full amount, then you may need to catch up before you can do anything else. If you cannot pay back your late payments, ask the creditor if you can work out a new payment plan that includes removal of the late payment information after you finish making a set number of payments, such as the first twelve monthly payments for the next year.

If they still want the full amount first, then you will have to get up to date on the amount owed. Once you are up to date with your payments, you can contact the creditor and plead your case to remove the negative late payment information. If you have a long-term relationship with them, let them know.

How to Get Credit Card Offers?

A clear majority of lenders don't have offers that are clearly defined up front, instead they have a general loan package that can be tweaked based on the situation individuals who come to them find themselves in. It becomes apparent why it is so important to seek out multiple offers before deciding.

To maximize this strategy, you are going to want to make a list of the features you are absolutely going to need to be happy with a given loan and then call each lender you have already talked to and go down the list point by point. If you come across a lender who has an approach that appeals to you, let the other lenders know about it and see what they can do to either match or beat it. They know they are in a competitive business and if you are willing to force their hand, they will show you just how much they want your business.

Pre-approved offers: If you have not opted out of the system, and your credit isn't terrible, then putting in an application with one lender will likely trigger a barrage of competing offers from other lenders as creditors will happily provide your information to anyone and everyone who is interested in selling you on their services.

While this can be annoying in some cases, if you are looking for the best lender possible then it could be just what you need to pit several lenders against one another. Pre-screened offers can make it easier for you to compare relative costs or special offers, as long as you do your due diligence with each and ensure that you aren't being hornswoggled by smoke and mirrors.

Ensure you have a loan estimate document: The loan estimate document was created by the Consumer Financial Protection Bureau to make it easier for borrowers to compare the various costs associated with individual loans and lenders. Its job is to standardize and simplify the way that lenders expose their fees so that you aren't comparing apples to oranges. The loan estimate document can be downloaded from ConsumerFinance.gov.

When and How to Open or Close a Credit Card

A major factor that plays into determining whether opening credit card accounts will be favorable to you or not is the credit utilization ratio. It is prudent to ensure that your credit utilization ratio is as low as possible. Essentially, you must make sure that you are using too much credit. You might be tempted to close certain credit card accounts, especially if you have managed to pay off all your credit card dues. However, don't do this. Don't allow the temptation to increase your spending get a hold of you. Your credit utilization ratio can increase when you close an account. So, if you don't trust yourself with a credit card, you can store it away for safekeeping or keep it out of your reach.

A Technique for Paying Off Your Credit Card Debt

If all your accounts have a similar interest rate, the Snowball Method might be a better option, but if you have one or two cards with a scandalously high interest rate, the Avalanche Method might be the right solution. It should be noted that both methods require that you have enough money to pay more than the minimum on your credit cards.

Avalanche method
Using this method, people use the extra money they get each month to pay off the debt at the highest interest rate, with all minimum payments remaining. By eliminating higher interest payments faster, you'll pay less interest over the next few months until the total debt is paid off. Once you have paid off your first high interest debt, find the next highest interest rate

and repeat the process. Pay above the minimum amount as much as you can, so you can get out of debt faster.

Snowball method

By following this method, people instead of focusing on the highest debt, should first focus on paying off the card with the lowest debt until they reach the largest regardless of the interest rate. Then you work your way so you can pay the most you owe.

Paying debts with the lowest amounts first, you pay off those smaller payments quickly and have fewer bills to worry about. Finally, you should continue to pay the bills with the lowest balances until you have no debt left.

Chapter 4.

Ways to Make and Save More Money with a High Credit Score

How to Use a Credit Card to Make Money and Earn Extra Cash

As you have all heard by now, you should maintain all your payments and keep low balances and you will live happily ever after. Yes, this is true and you will get all that you deserve with a good foundation of credit like pre-approvals, more credit card solicitations than you actually want, and automatic credit line increases on your current credit card accounts, but that is not it. Once you get to this point, most so-called credit experts will stop giving you the advice that will take your credit to the next level. You have to be aware that with higher credit card limits and access to cash, you will be tempted in more ways than one and this could possibly be dangerous to the immature and undisciplined individual.

Primary Tradelines VS Authorized User Tradelines

When you think of boosting your credit score, the key word in this process will be trade lines. During the process of building or rebuilding your credit you applied for starter credit cards or maybe even a secured credit card or two. The credit cards or accounts you obtained during the building process is very critical to your success in developing a solid credit file. You can't have good credit without having positive reporting trade lines, especially revolving credit lines such as credit cards. Any account that you got approved for on your own is considered a PRIMARY ACCOUNT, you are the primary account holder and you hold all responsibilities for that account. AUTHORIZED USER TRADELINES exist only when a primary account holder adds a person to their credit card account.

Most major credit card companies allow any primary account holder to add up to 5 authorized users to their credit card account regardless of the credit limit. With this action, the account holder can control and designate how much access each authorized user can have or how long they choose to keep them on the account. Each time the creditor updates any activity related to the account with the credit bureaus for the primary account holder, they will report the exact same information for the authorized users of that account regardless of their responsibility for the account; including any late payments, balances and even credit line increases. The age of the account will also be reported as a benefit to the authorized user. The backdated payment activity is the most beneficial feature of being added as an AU, the authorized user adopts the years' worth of positive payments, if you get added to a credit card account as an authorized user that is 10 years old, your credit reports will reflect that you have made on-time payments for this account for 10 years, even if you were just recently added to the account. Beware, this tactic can backfire if the primary account holder has missed payments or normally carries balances higher than 30%, the authorized users will also pay the price of the negative information.

AU Tradelines

A primary credit card account is more favorable than an AUTHORIZED USER ACCOUNT as some computer systems and underwriters take into consideration the illusion that authorized user accounts can have when the fico score is being generated. AU accounts can still be a very dangerous weapon for you to use, lenders have caught on to this technique as people would take a totally naked credit file, add 3 or 4 authorized user trade lines to the file, then apply for funding with the newly accumulated 700 plus credit scores. Understand that AU trade lines are still very effective, but you have to do a little more work to blend them into your credit boosting strategies. With the help of authorized user trade lines, it is very easy to get a "useless" 700-800 credit score that you will have a hard time getting the approvals for, even getting approved for the most basic cards can be difficult. It is very important to build your credit out the proper way to avoid a thin credit file with a high fico score, you will be very disappointed as you rake up inquiries just to keep getting denied. Therefore, building a foundation is very important and you should not skip the starter credit cards.

Ideally you will want a fresh credit file with no negatives reporting which should have been your goal during the repair process. Once you finished your credit repair or if you are just beginning to build your credit for the first time, you will need to get approved for at least 2-3 primary trade lines to start with, I recommend you let those primary trade lines age for at least 4-5 months before applying for anything else. Once you have maintained 2-3 primary accounts, you can add 2 authorized user trade lines with some age and decent credit limits. With each Au trade line being 5 years or older in age, and with limits of at least $10,000, you will be in a good position to secure your next level of primary accounts. You want to get away from those Level 1 starter credit cards with small limits of $500-$1,000 and get to the point where all approvals will be Levels 3 and 4 with $5,000 to $10,000 limits and above, this will be considered your first round of primary accounts. This is the proper position for a nice build-out of your credit file; I would suggest you obtain 2 or 3 approvals on this round at those limits. Every credit card you apply for now should be a credit card from a major issuer, American Express, Capital One, Discover, Citi bank, Chase, or Credit Unions as they are more generous with approvals and credit limits.

The older the accounts, the better they are for everyone, as your primary credit accounts are aging, you should be learning. You can get in position to help your family build credit or start your own community of credit for investment purposes without having to ask others for help. How powerful can you be when your whole family has perfect credit?

Typically, unless you get added as an Authorized user from a family member or a friend, people will want to charge you as the strategy of piggybacking on other people's positive credit accounts has become well known. It's standard for people to pay to be added to positive aged trade lines, companies exist and thrive on brokering these positive accounts to clients who need a boost in credit for funding purposes. This practice is 100% legal. The primary account holder can add authorized users by simply calling their credit card companies.

Find Out the Ways to Make and Save Money

Handling Addiction to Overspending

Overspending for them isn't the problem but a consequence of the actual problems which can range from a desire to escape negative feelings or stressful situations to the urge to fill a gaping void left by unmet needs.

Let's look at the first psychological trigger for shopaholics: the desire to escape negative feelings. This trigger is prevalent in several cases of addiction. An impulsive buyer overspends for the same reason a chronic alcoholic cannot stop or doesn't want to stop after having a few bottles: to drown out the noise from the world. In other words, to escape an unpleasant reality and find momentary happiness.

For a shopaholic, the path to this addiction can be very innocuous. It could easily have started as a lady's friends coming around to take her shopping after she suffered a nasty breakup. She succumbs and then discovers. Her new acquisitions weren't going to reject her as her boyfriend did; they are hers forever. So, she goes home feeling much better. She soon discovers that her mind keeps digging up memories of her experience at the mall, and she subscribes to that therapy whenever she feels bad. Soon, all she can think of is burying her worries beneath several shopping sprees.

Several feelings addicts seek an escape from include depression, pain from the loss of a loved one, family crisis, and a host of others.

For some others, shopping can serve as plugs to clog voids created by unmet needs. Consider the case of a neglected trophy wife. She probably finds joy in hanging out with friends but discovers that the joy doubles when she's out throwing her husband's money around. The things she acquires, the people she's able to connect with because of her "generosity" are all emotional void fillers.

We've taken this short trip through the mind of an average shopaholic so you can see that the problem cannot be solved by simply taking their credit cards away, I mean, are you saying they would never have access to them again? This beast needs to be taken down from below, from its roots, permanently.

Winning the Battle Against Shopping Addiction

Having established that addiction to shopping, which leads to overspending, is caused by the same root triggers of other forms of addiction, it is logical to conclude that the same methods used in dealing with these forms of addiction should prove effective in handling overspending. That aside, it is widely known that the predominant and most effective method of treating addiction is therapy.

With reports suggesting that between 5% and 9% of Americans have compulsive shopping disorders, finding help as a compulsive or impulsive spender isn't difficult at all. Addiction counsellors are on the ground, and a good number of therapeutic interventions are being applied in helping addicts, including cognitive-behavioral therapy (CBT) and the 12-step program.

Cognitive-behavioral therapy looks to hijack the power of overspending by helping the addict challenge delusional beliefs, which are widely regarded as building blocks for the triggers of compulsive spending. Thoughts are believed to be sponsors of emotions and behaviors. CBT uses this assertion to attempt to assist addicts in influencing their feelings about shopping and remodeling their shopping behaviors by first reshaping their thoughts about the activity and getting their minds in the right place. This has been a very successful intervention program in treating many addictive behaviors.

The age of the account will also be reported as a benefit to the authorized user, even if you were just recently added to the account. Beware, this tactic can backfire if the primary account holder normally carries balances higher than 30%, the authorized users will also pay the price of the negative information.

While cognitive-behavioral therapy is majorly characterized by a single patient interacting with a trained therapist at regular intervals, group cognitive therapy is a more effective treatment for shopping addiction. This is perhaps due to the additional benefits that accompany being in a group of people battling the same problem. Addicts find themselves in a community of people who understand what they are faced with and can relate with them without being judgmental. Thoughts and struggles are shared freely, and burdens are borne communally. This helps a great deal in speeding up the healing process.

Plausible measures for putting your spending under control:

- Take someone with you when you shop.
- Put your credit cards out of your reach.
- Unsubscribe from retailer emails
- Don't hang out around malls and retail stores
- Use automated savings systems or apps

TIPS AND TRICS

Raise Your Credit Score

Chapter 5.

Tips and Tricks to Raise Your Credit Score and Get 730+ Point

It is quite understandable that a person's creditworthiness can only be determined by the numbers he added to his name in this age of numbers game. A prospective loan applicant's proposal must be rejected if it has not yet reached a respectable base number of 700. A person's total loan count reflects the applicant's ability to disburse the prospective lender if the proposal is accepted.

The number of loans usually varies between 340 and 850. The applicant's lack of respectable creditworthiness may be the reason why an application is rejected or, even if accepted, must increase an interest rate that would make it above average to compensate the creditor in question. Some people find it uncomfortable not to have serious credit because they are unable to pay their bills and debts in full.

The lack of creditworthiness forces some to prepare for the worst by purchasing Master or Visa cards and credit cards for department stores only based on their pay slips. Keep the appropriate records of your electricity bills before paying them all, as well as the invoices of all items that were intentionally purchased on credit to obtain a significant number. By overcoming all impulses for conspicuous consumption and instantly repaying bills of essential items, people in the United States are planning their financial operations to get good credit because they understand the importance of good credit that will not be compromised.

An impressive credit score can be achieved not only by planning transactions that add valuable points to the score but also by avoiding purchases where points are deducted to neutralize the advantage. It is often inconvenient for people to raise funds when they are unable to increase the monthly payment schedule, knowing that they cannot withstand the pressure, the eventuality of which on reasonably decent number 1 score would influence the favorable terms.

To keep the score reasonably decent, the borrower is forced to seek a new loan that goes beyond official records and that a lender can accept by charging a higher interest rate. Too many credit cards mean too many small balances, which means too many irrelevant allocations of the debtor's credit-related activities, which cannot contribute to the accumulation/improvement. Therefore, it is advisable to cancel the cards and keep only two cards that have the longest history and the lowest interest rate.

Before three years of credit history, you shouldn't make the usual mistake of opening a new account if there is no obligation. You should get into the habit of turning credit updating on and off, especially when you approach 700. Correcting all errors in your credit report should be effective by forwarding the error with support to the agency in the matter, the documents that can control and act.

The unlikely magic number of the loan, e.g. H. 700 or higher, can be achieved by increasing efforts to maintain it. Once there, you can take advantage of loans at reduced interest rates, which can differ, for example, for tuition fees for renovating a house and buying houses or cars.

One should be competent enough to use creditworthiness to determine the possibility of a loan, which would surely save him a lot of time, energy, money and perhaps embarrassment.

Next on the list is to find ways that you can limit the liability that you are dealing with. When you go to co-sign a loan, remember that this may seem like a nice thing to do, but you are really taking on a risk for another person. If you do this for someone who is not able to manage their debt all that well, it is going to negatively affect your score because you will be responsible for that debt as well. if you want to make sure that you can get a credit score that is 800+, and maintain that, then it is a good idea to avoid co-signing at all.

In addition to this one, you should make sure that your liability is limited in other manners as well. You should always report your cards that have been lost or stolen right away. If you don't do this, then it is likely that you will be liable for any of the purchases that are not authorized at the time. And if you are not able to afford those purchases, then your score is going to be the thing that suffers here.

And finally, we need to make sure that we are restricting the hard inquiries that happen to our report. Whether it is you or another agency or institution who is pulling out the credit report and asking for a copy of it, you are dealing with an inquiry. A soft inquiry can happen on occasion as well, and it is generally not going to be enough to make any changes to your credit. This soft inquiry is going to happen when one of the following occurs:

1. You go through and do a check on your own credit report.
2. You give an employer you may work with in the future permission to go through and check your credit.
3. You have the financial institutions that you do business with go through and check your credit.
4. You get a credit card offer that has been preapproved, and that specific company goes through and checks your credit.

While the soft inquiry is not going to do all that much to our credit scores, we do need to be careful about the hard inquiry. This is going to be the one that is able to affect your credit score. It is when a company is going to pull up your credit report after you apply for a product like a credit card or a mortgage. You want to make sure that you can limit the hard inquiries as much as possible to get the best results with this.

Will Debt Consolidation Hurt My Score in a Negative Way?

Simply put, this means putting all your debts into one account, meaning you will owe money to only to one credit institution and pay them only once a month (or bi-weekly or weekly depending on what you negotiate). In the process, your new creditor will pay off your current creditors, meaning you now owe all your debt to this one new creditor. The idea behind this is that your new interest rate will be lower than the combined interest rate you had before, meaning you can pay off your debt quicker, because more of your money is going towards paying off your capital instead of going straight into interest. It also makes things much simpler and less stressful for you since having just one payment to worry about is much less to think about and easier to budget for than several throughout the month.

That will give you the lowest interest rate. However, depending on where you are in time with your mortgage term, it can come with some very high fees which may more than account for any interest saved. Remortgaging might also not provide you with enough cash to pay off all your other debts. So, here we will look at the process of debt consolidation for any remaining debts and how to decide on the best plan of attack for your situation.

Other considerations for debt consolidation

Whilst finding the lowest interest rate is the most important thing here, there are a few other considerations that are very important when negotiating to consolidate your debts:

1. Sometimes financial institutions will only allow you to have a lower rate when it is combined with a longer repayment period. This means that even though you are paying less in interest every month, you will pay more over the long term than you would have before you consolidated. This is because you are paying it off over a longer period than you would have before. So, even though your monthly payments are lower, you are in fact paying more over the long term, which really defies the point of consolidating in the first place. This really buys you some wiggle room financially in the short term but is really hurting you more in the long term.

2. Sometimes financial institutions will put restrictions on how much and how often you can pay off extra amounts. This can be really frustrating as occasionally you may come into some extra cash (maybe an annual bonus, a small inheritance, or some extra overtime). When you are committed to paying off your debt as quickly as possible, the obvious (and sensible) thing to do is put the extra money towards paying off your debt. However, many people come unstuck as they didn't consider this when signing with their debt consolidator. Remember, the financial institutions want you to pay it off over as longer period as possible to maximize their profit. They might be pretty sneaky with this so always be clear with them

as to what you want and read the contract carefully. This is also important because if you don't have the option to pay off any lump sum along the course of your repayment schedule, it means you are effectively forced to pay off a slightly lower amount than you think you can afford each month, because there are always unexpected life events that you can't budget for, especially if you paying it off over many years. You always need some wiggle room throughout the duration of your debt repayment. Situations always change in unexpected ways.

Know common mistakes and avoid them

Chapter 6.

Most Common Errors Found in Credit Reports and How to Avoid Them

According to the federal trade commission, 1 in 5 Americans has a mistake on their credit report. In other words, approximately 40 million Americans have an error on their credit report; this number is not only astounding, but it is very revealing. Therefore, a lot of people are being denied credit based on inaccurate information found on their credit file. Also, some people are paying high-interest rates based on errors found that were found in their credit reports.

Three common mistakes that cause errors on credit reports

- Sometimes people inadvertently provide the wrong social security number when applying for credit.
- People at times make a mistake when they enter your information on a credit application.
- An account that belong to John Smith Sr. sometimes will get reported as owned by John Smith Jr.

Note that there could be various mistakes in each of the three credit reports. It is not uncommon to have positive coverage of an account on one article, but poor reports on another.

Here are others of the most common credit report errors.

- Listed wrong names, emails, or phone numbers.
- Data that refers to another of the same name.
- Duplicate details, whether positive or negative, about the same account.
- Records have negative, apparently positive information.
- Balances on accounts payable are still on view.
- Delinquent payment reports that were never billed in due time.
- This indicates wrong credit limits.
- Claims included in the insolvency which are still due.
- Incorrect activity dates.
- Past-due payments not payable.
- Court records which are falsely connected with you, such as convictions and bankruptcy.
- Tax liens not yours.
- Unprecedented foreclosures.
- Incorrect names
- Wrong address
- Wrong social security number
- Accounts NOT belonging to you

- Accounts with the incorrect credit limit
- Open accounts being reported as closed
- Closed accounts being reported as open
- Account incorrectly reported as being late
- Out-dated information
- The mixture of the two different credit reports
- Identity theft
- An account listed twice
- Incorrect phone number
- Authorized user listed as the owner of an account
- Ex-spouse information listed on credit report
- Incorrect account status

How to Prevent Common Errors on Your Credit Report?

It can be very disheartening to discover that you might have errors on your credit report but taking steps to prevent errors from being placed on your credit report can help you to avoid a lot of unnecessary stress. Take extra caution to secure yourself against identity theft. You should consider setting up credit monitoring alerts to inform you whenever a recent update has been made to your credit report, act fast to correct any errors on your credit report and double check any information you provide to a creditor when you apply for credit. Many times, if you have had a long-term account with a creditor, you can contact them directly and explain the error being reported on your credit report.

Ask them to write you a letter with the email and correction. Also ask them to contact every credit reporting agency that reports this incorrect entry in order to make the correction.

Once the creditor receives a copy of the letter, make a copy of it, and attach the letter to the letter of dispute you send. Mail it to the agency for credit reporting and ask them to update their files. Once that is completed, you will be sent back a new credit report by the credit reporting agency.

Chapter 7.

Managing Debt

Your credit use rate or the aggregate sum of accessible debt utilized on your accounts (unsecured and secured) is the second biggest factor toward obtaining a solid credit score. Beside your verified debt, which is paid down according to a calendar and doesn't increase in the amount owed, we should concentrate here on uncollateralized debt, which is the costliest debt and furthermore, the debt that is least demanding to gain out of power. In case you're overpowered with debt or have burrowed a huge gap from which you're uncertain how to begin moving out, my first advice is to unwind. There is absolutely no motivation to experience the ill effects of superfluous uneasiness or stress in light of debt. Losing rest and agonizing night and day over fortuitous debt won't assist you with receiving in return, so accept the way that you are in debt and start considering how and when you can receive in return.

Credit Card Debt is the Costliest Debt
Credit card debt is the most choking out debt of all, and the feeling of always digging and getting no place is a feeling to which I can relate very well. Don't

give it a chance to make you crazy. With an activity plan and being persevering not to overextend yourself, you can gradually arrive at a point where your credit card debt is neither bringing you nor your credit score down. While I'm not a specialist in credit card debt guiding.

I realize that in my circumstance, I had the option to toss little lumps of my compensation at this pile of debt — a few months in bigger pieces, others in littler pieces—until I had a little enough balance to clear out. While this segment intends to provide some accommodating tips on the most proficient method to manage your debt, if that you believe you are absolutely up the creek without a paddle, or a significant life event, for example, joblessness, or a medicinal issue or anything is preventing you from having the option to pay down any of your debt, at that point jumping to the following segment might be progressively appropriate for you.

Debt Management Tips

For those of you who are in the limbo period of, "Should I pay-down debt," or "Should I file bankruptcy," comprehend that there are two types of personal bankruptcy: the main, Bankruptcy, takes into consideration most or the entirety of your debts to be discharged or dropped. The second, known as Bankruptcy, plans your debt for repayment over some stretch of time. If that you are thinking about both two choices, at that point it is highly recommended that you search out somebody with mastery, for example, a bankruptcy trustee or lawyer. Sometimes everything necessary is a professional's advice and helping hand to guide you the correct way. If you are going to attempt to dig yourself out of debt without documenting personal bankruptcy or choosing your debts for not exactly the aggregate sum owed with your creditors, you have to have a plan.

What's the Best Approach to Deal with Huge Credit Card Debt?

There is no uncertainty that the interest on credit card debt can be an executioner. Many credit cards have interest rates more than 20%. If you utilize Chris' Debt Repayment Calculator (at welker.ca) you can perceive the amount it will cost to pay off your credit cards with interest more than five years. Perhaps the biggest error that people make when they are attempting to dig themselves out of debt all alone is making payments that simply spread the interest charges yet aren't really lessening the head.

Chris Walker says that if you are battling to deal with your credit card debt and you need to pay back what you can bear, at that point the best alternative may be a consumer proposal for a repayment. By offering a consumer proposal, you can stop interest charges, prevent creditor collection activity, and settle your debt. While documenting a consumer proposal briefly damages your credit rating, it is frequently the best approach for people dealing with huge credit card debt. Don't make the mistake of concentrating on your credit rating. While credit rating is important, improving your financial wellbeing is undeniably progressively important. You can generally modify your credit rating, yet If that you don't have a plan to escape debt you will continue to battle.

If You Need to Manage Your Credit Card APRs

In cases of medical or employment hardships, or some other setbacks in life, creditors will sometimes permit a decrease or freeze on additional fund charges to your existing debt. Everything necessary is calling to discover what they can do subsequent to disclosing to them your circumstance—it might be critical enough to accommodate their explanation codes or extraordinary programs. Creditors frequently save these for people who might be not able make timely payments or the full amount of the average monthly payments due, and the programs may keep going for set time periods of six months to a year or more.

In return for enrolling in these programs, a few creditors may likewise stop your account preventing you from making additional buys and adding to your existing debt. Obviously, you won't realize what options you have until you call, so in case you're reluctant about grabbing the telephone, discover the time to call every one of your creditors and examine these options which could bring some truly necessary help. Inquire as to whether you can make a lesser monthly payment. This would be your most solid option If that you are as yet ready to manage a smidgen of a monthly payment, notwithstanding any plans for a DIY debt settlement. You'll be happy you called — anything to help diminish the amount of interest charged and APRs consistently. The goal here is to get what, assuming any, options you have, at managing or keeping your balances low. Twofold check that by enrolling yourself in any diminished APR or APR-freezing programs, creditors will continue reporting to the CRAs that you are making timely payments. (Creditors can begin reporting harsh payments if a bill is 30days overdue.)

Settling Your Own Debts

While personal debt settlement was to a great extent a totally unbelievable practice as meagre as five years back, a plenty of DIY debt pilgrims have now taken their accounts of the process to online media and web journals. More news and research on the subject, by and large, has additionally now put the process inside go after the individuals who wish to take the creditors head-on. Many have picked this course to be in all out control of their settlement process as opposed to enlisting an outsider debt arbitrator to intercede. You can settle your debts all alone; anyway, you should be prepared and solid willed. You'll need to suffer and confront creditors' and debt collectors' endeavors and strategies at getting you to pay up, which can be out and out forceful and smooth. Furthermore, you will must be sorted out at managing and monitoring the results of each arranged account. People are procured by organizations to make debt collection their full-time exertion and are compensated accordingly, so don't overlook they are professionals at endeavoring to get anything they can out of any debtor.

Debt settlement is positively an option for any individual who basically can't make payments or who has fallen so behind that the subsequent stage would resort bankruptcy. An outline of personal debt settlement includes:

1. Halting any payments on every uncollateralized debt that you can't pay. Right away.

2. Pausing and avoiding creditors as they attempt to chase you down to collect their outstanding payments. If that they have your telephone number, it is alright getting another PDA saved for loved ones. The goal is released the account until it gets so

far financially past due that they will be desperate to settle with you before charging off the account.

3. Proposing a debt settlement for as meager as 20 percent on the amount you owe. This may require some intense arrangement and standing your ground.

4. Affirming everything in writing from the creditor regarding any debt settlement and payback terms. It is prudent to not fall for a reset of the process by sending in any cash until you have, in your grasp, the creditor's letter plotting the terms which are agreeable to you.

Once more, personal debt settlement isn't for everybody. Debt settlement will assuredly damage your credit when creditors and collection agencies continue reporting reprobate payments on your accounts.

You'll get a good deal on any charges you'd pay debt directing or combination organizations to consult for your sake. Likewise, you may have an easier time with creditors, since your creditors and collectors will realize they're dealing straightforwardly with you rather than an agent, who might be harder to work with. Creditors may go easier on you.

Chapter 8.

Identity Theft

Did you ever wonder if people are becoming the perpetrators of identity theft? Or maybe you have been and you're not sure how it happened. There are plenty of approaches used by hackers to get your personal information a hold.

Theft of identity is one form of fraud. It is defined as taking or claiming the identity of another person to use existing accounts, open new credit accounts or receive other benefits for a fraudulent reason from their personal information. A person's credit cards are usually used for making purchases. Social Security cards and numbers were also taken to establish new credit in your name.

How Identity Theft Happens

Identity theft happens in a variety of ways; hackers obtain access to your personal information by removing it from your purse or wallet, impersonating an official representative and accessing your identity through the mail and computer technology. Here are some of the way's identity thieves get your personal data:

- **Skimming**. Occasionally there may be a special storage device connected to the card reader while you swipe your credit card or debit card during a normal transaction. This system collects and stores up to several hundred numbers per credit card at a time. When you transfer the details to a computer, the identity thief will have access to your information without even realizing it.

- **Hacking**. Most identity thieves are also hackers. For businesses that have personal records for place, they will use smart technology to hack into your personal computers or computer systems. Many banks were also victims of malware and all of their clients may have been victims of identity theft.

- **Stealing** mail. The e-mail provides credit card statements, tax information, bank statements, credit deals pre-approved and even new checks. Thieves will rob from your mailbox right away and were even known to have mail sent to them. This confidential information is at their disposal and can help them rob their identities.

- **Dumpster** diving. Identity thieves also rummage through your personal garbage, something that often occurs in companies. Robbers search and locate bank account numbers, credit card numbers, financial statements and other personal information through the trash.

- **Stealing purses and wallets**. Often, identity thieves rummage through your personal trash, something that sometimes occurs in companies. Thieves dig through the garbage for and find bank account numbers, credit card numbers, financial statements and other personal data.

- **Employees of businesses.** Identity thieves can sometimes steal personal records from businesses. This could be an employee's role taking company documents from his or her own boss in order to gain access to confidential information. Many identity thieves at a business may conspire with an employee who can give them access to personal records. Therefore, workers receiving credit reports can violate their rights to that information.

- **E-mails and phone calls.** Identity hackers were known to impersonate your broker, trustee or other company representative by calling or giving you an e-mail. Do not do so if you receive a mysterious phone call or e-mail demanding your personal information to either check your account or to claim money. They most likely try to steal your credit card number, Social Security number, or other account numbers, whatever the scheme.

- **Home theft.** Many robbers are trying to break into your home not to steal your Television or jewels, but to take your name. They will steal tax information, bank account numbers, Social Security numbers, number of credit card accounts and any other personal information they might discover.

What to Do If You Are a Victim of Identity Theft

Have you ever seen this happen? You just received a collection notice in the mail for an account you didn't use or even know about, you received a credit card in the mail you never wanted or opened, or you were simply turned down for a loan or credit card due to a low FICO score with accounts that weren't even yours. If there has been one of these cases, you are most likely a victim of identity theft.

You might feel robbed, betrayed and left wondering how this might happen to you. Your credit scores were most likely impacted negatively. You may need a loan or credit, and this condition prohibits you from receiving it. To fix the damage that has already happened and to mitigate potential future harm, you need to take control and figure out what to do next.

Criminal laws regulate identity theft. According to the Identity Theft and Assumption Deterrence Act of 1998, it is a felony to "consciously pass or use, without legal authority, a means of identifying another person with the intention of committing, or aiding or abetting, any criminal conduct that constitutes a breach of Federal law or that constitutes a crime under any State or local statute applicable." The law is in place to provide offenders with a consolidated complaint process, as well as improve the criminal laws surrounding identity theft. If you're a victim of identity theft, prompt action is required. The law allows claimants to challenge unauthorized charges; however, there are some time-limits that need to be followed.

- **Notify the creditor.** When you find unauthorized charges on your credit or debit card, then you were most likely a victim of identity theft. The good news is that the Equal Credit Billing Act limits any responsibility for unauthorized charges to $50. When you discover the unauthorized charges, you will have to write down your trustee, disputing the questionable payments.

Write the letter of disagreement to the agency "Billing inquiries" of your creditor. Make sure you send the certified letter to your trustee and you know it's hitting you. Notify the creditor as soon as the unwanted payment is identified and make sure that your letter hits them within 60 days of the first bill revealing the mistake. Keep yourself a copy of the letter. Under statute, the creditor must respond within 30 days of receiving the message, and the conflict must be settled within two billing cycles.

- **Notify your bank.** If your debit card has been stolen, you will report it to your bank within two working days. Under the Electronic Fund Transfer Act, you will only be held liable for $50 in unauthorized charges; however, you will be responsible for $500 of unauthorized charges if you report the unauthorized charges between three and 60 days. Unless you wait until 60 days later, you can lose all of the money stolen from your account. If your debit card has a Visa or MasterCard mark, both firms will limit your liabilities to $50 per card in unauthorized charges.

It's better that you alert your suppliers and banks as soon as you can or your debit cards, credit cards and even personal checks have been stolen if you detect fraudulent charges. The longer you wait to contact the lender, the greater the chance that some or all of the unauthorized charges will be placed on you.

- **Fraud alert**. If you've been a victim of identity theft, it's important to create a warning about fraud. If you call credit reporting agencies, you will have to choose between two different types of fraud alerts- the expanded warning and the original notice.

The expanded notice entitles you to receive two free credit reports from each credit reporting agency per year; however, for seven years, the fraud alert must stay on your register. The most common type of warning against fraud is the original alarm. This will live 90 days on your file and will send you one free credit report from each of the three reporting agencies.

You must have a police report and evidence of the theft or attempted fraud to create an extended warning. You may request that for your protection, only the last four digits of your Social Security number appear on your credit report. You may also cancel any warning about fraud at any time.

To set up a fraud alert for your own protection is in your best interest. This means the robber can't open credit in your name. You will notify the other credit reporting offices whether you call one of the credit reporting agencies to set up the fraud alert.

Your credit report and credit score are important to you and to your future earnings. Make sure you check them regularly to ensure you're not a victim of identity theft.

- **Police report**. If you suspect that you are a victim of identity theft, it is in your best interests to lodge a police report. Some creditors may require that a police report be used as evidence of the incident. Many police stations hesitate to take a call on identity theft. Assure your submission is permanent. Make sure that you have a copy of the report for your history, because credit card companies and banks may need to see the report and search for unauthorized charges. Remember, make sure that you have the name and phone number of the prosecutor, in case the investors need to talk to him or her.
- **Social Security Administration**. If your Social Security card has been stolen or you know your Social Security number has been used to open new accounts, you will call the Department of Social Security. They will most of the time issue you a new Social Security number and card. To apply for a new Social Security number, you must provide evidence that someone using your account is still harming you. Your sex, U.S. residency, or legal immigration status, and name will need to be confirmed.
- **Postal inspector**. When you believe that your mail was robbed or sent to a different location, you were most likely a victim of identity theft in which a criminal rummaged through your mail or used a Change of Address form to give them your mail. Contact the postal inspector for documentation and prosecute this fraud.

- **Department of Motor Vehicles**. If you have stolen your driver's license, you need to contact your state agency that issued your license. Most of the time, you can locate their contact information by checking the Department of Motor Vehicles in your state online. They will cancel your license and give you instructions on how to get another license.
- **Federal Trade Commission**. You will report the crime to the Federal Trade Commission (FTC) if you've been a victim of identity theft. Call them at IDTHEFT (877), or at www.idtheft.gov. Although the FTC does not prosecute identity theft, it exchanges concerns with local regulatory bodies that support the federal fight against identity theft.

Chapter 9.

How Credit System Works

In a nutshell, the entire credit system constitutes the credit bureaus, the creditors and you. Creditors are the companies you access credit from while the credit bureaus collect credit data from past and current creditors and compile it into reports, which are modelled in the form of credit profiles for each credit consumer, after which they sell these reports to creditors so that they can make various decisions.

The creditors use the data they obtain from credit bureaus to determine how much they will charge you for borrowing and the amount of penalties they should charge you for defaulting. Whenever a creditor needs credit profiles of people that have a certain credit score, they buy that information from the credit bureaus. This helps them to target their products and services since they will then send emails to those in that list enticing them to buy or use their products and services. It is believed that most of these companies go after those that have a low score. This will allow them to have a chance at making a greater profit and pulling out as much money as possible from these people's pockets.

Get to Know Credit System

The credit system consists of three parties namely you, the creditors, and the credit bureaus.

If a creditor needs a report of credit consumers who have a specific credit score, they can then buy the credit profiles from the credit bureaus thus making it easy to target products and services appropriately. They (creditors) will send you enticing information on offers that you should buy.

Subprime credit data is the best-selling for the different credit reporting agencies. Therefore, if you have a subprime credit rating, you are likely to be getting countless email solicitations for you to apply to different credit cards. The reasoning for this is straight forward. With a subprime credit rating, you are going to be charged more for accessing credit. This simply means that the lenders will make more money from you. If you have excellent credit rating, you are low risk and lenders charge you less for accessing credit, which means that they make less money when they advance your credit. In other terms, lenders will want to prey on you if you have bad credit because they are certain that they will make more money in the end. Even if you are to default, you are likely to have paid more money than someone who has good credit!

Subprime data is such a hot selling product that the credit reporting agencies charge more for it; it is in high demand! This can be translated to mean that the creditors and credit bureaus don't care about you having good credit. In any case, if your credit rating is bad, they will charge you more! Do you know that over 90 per cent of credit reports have been proven to have inaccurate, unverifiable, and erroneous entries?

Well, now you know why your credit score is always becoming bad even with all your effort. These companies are in it for profit. They will even overlook when erroneous entries are posted in your report. In any case, they have convinced us to think that the reports are the gospel truth when they are nowhere close to that. So, in simple terms, these 2 players in the credit system can only be compelled by the law to put things in order. They have no interest in you having perfect credit because they all make more money if you have bad credit.

If you are in this group of credit consumers, you will get the most enticing offers and email solicitations to apply for credit cards. The reason is simple, as was mentioned, when your credit score isn't so good, the creditors will charge more for advancing your credit, which means that they make more money. In financial terms, creditors address their exposure to credit risk through charging more for credit. If you have the capacity to pay the right amount on time this will cause them to lose out on a substantial amount of profit. They will not be satisfied with what they receive and will want more out of their customers. They might not directly refuse you credit but will not be particularly interested in giving you money. They will be waiting for someone with bad credit to walk in. When you have poor credit, you might be paying up to three times what you would pay were you to have a perfect credit score.

So, the companies will expressly go after those that have a bad score and will put in all possible effort to trap them. As you can see, creditors will be inclined to prey on those with sub-prime credit score for the simple reason that they will make more money from them even if they were to default as they will have made money already! So, there is a lot of planning that they do just to fill up their pockets.

It should not surprise you that these companies work hand in hand. It takes effort from both ends for their schemes to work and they will ensure that they are on the same page. They will come up with plans that will benefit both and cause each to make a large profit at the expense of the customer. Imagine trying to cheat millions of customers on a yearly basis, it is a Herculean task and will require the company to be as prepared as possible to pull it off with ease. For this reason, they will join hands and make sure each one cuts into the profit.

Apart from these 2, there will be some third parties who will work to help these credit companies. These can be outsourced companies or independent ones looking to hook up with the credit companies and trying to make money for themselves. These will have the exclusive job of looking for people that have not checked their records for some time and determine to get them on board. They will put in a lot of effort to catch these people's fancy and once they trap them, they will direct them to the credit company and get them to pay for their services.

To prove that your bad credit history records are a best seller for credit reporting agencies, do you know that they will even charge more to credit providers to access such information. That's right, they will pay up a little extra just to find those that have a bad credit and start bombarding them with emails that ask them to apply for credit at their place. This means that none of these parties has any specific interest to have the information in your credit report reported accurately.

Do you know that only a small percentage of people file disputes for such items despite over 90 per cent of credit reports having been found to have erroneous, unverifiable and inaccurate entries? Many will not wish to go through the pain of proving themselves right. This allows the companies to have a long leash and they will not back away from exploiting these people. The companies have several good field days owing to such ignorance on the part of the customers.

The credit companies will be determined to report your bad credit and this means that some of them will even let such entries be included in your credit report for the simple reason that so few of us have the guts to challenge entries in the credit report even if they are incorrect, unverifiable and erroneous. They will know who exactly will not challenge it just by looking at your credit history. They will not have an interest in catering to those that might take up a dispute. They will employ people to especially look for those customers that have a bad score and those that look most likely to remain mum about errors in their reports.

The 2 other players in the credit system (the creditors and the credit reporting agencies) are in it to make the most money from you directly or indirectly so counting on them to help you make things right should be out of the question. The more screwed up your credit score is, the more money there is to be made by the credit reporting agencies and the creditors. That is, the lower the score, the better their prospects to charge you a bomb.

> *If you have a subprime credit rating you are likely to be getting countless email solicitations for you to apply to different credit cards. With a subprime credit rating, you are going to be charged more for accessing credit, because the lenders will make more money from you. In other terms, lenders will want to prey on you if you have bad credit because they are certain that they will make more money in the end.*

So, when you file a dispute, the creditors and the credit reporting agencies will only update the data - not because they have any interest in your welfare - but because they don't have an option given to them and they are under legal obligation to act in accordance with the law. They will not expressly pursue your cause and, in fact, despite your efforts to fix your bad score, they will try and remain ignorant of it and make things worse for you. They will go to any lengths just to make sure that you have no chance of fixing your score despite none of it being your fault.

This is the exact reason why there are hundreds, probably thousands, of people who despise credit card companies. They will not stop at anything and fall to the absolute lows just to make a few extra dollars. Many of these companies will have a bad reputation and yet find easy prey for themselves. They will know how exactly they can target the customers and get them to subscribe to their card. Once the person is trapped, they will not stop until they fulfil their desire to make as much money as possible. The poor customer will be trapped and will have to surrender to the demands of the vicious company.

Every day, there are hundreds of innocent customers who fall for this trick and do not put in the effort to check their credit reports. But it is important for every person to thoroughly go through their report and look for any erroneous and wrong entries that may be causing them their low scores.

Now that you understand that only yourself is on your side on matters pertaining the accuracy of the credit report, how do you know how your credit score affects your ability to borrow? It is apparent that your score is the most vital element in your report and something that needs to be investigated carefully. But what is this score and what are its parameters? How do you know that your score is good, average or bad?

Of course, the report doesn't state that a certain amount is bad, so understanding what benchmarks the lenders are going to use in categorizing you as good (perfect), average (sub-prime) and bad will be very helpful so that you know what to expect when you see that number on your credit report.

Let's Debunk Some Myth

Chapter 10.

Credit Scoring Myth

For a large portion of credit scoring's history, by far, most of the people engaged with loaning decisions pretty much needed to think about what hurt or helped a score. Makers of scoring formulas would not like to uncover much about how the models functioned, for dread that contenders would take their thoughts or that consumers would make sense of how to beat the framework. Luckily, today we discover much increasingly about credit scoring—however, not every person has stayed aware of the latest knowledge. Mortgage intermediaries, loan officials, credit agency agents, credit guides, and the media, among others, continue to spread outdated and out and out bogus information. Following up on their terrible guidance can put your score and your accounts at critical risk.

Here are probably the most widely recognized fantasies.

Myth 1: Closing Credit Accounts Will Help Your Score

This one sounds sensible, particularly when a mortgage merchant discloses to you that lenders are suspicious of people who have heaps of unused credit accessible to them. All What's you, all things considered, from hurrying out and charging up a tempest? Obviously, looking at the situation objectively, what's shielded you from piling on huge balances before now? If you've been responsible with credit before, you're probably going to continue to be responsible later. That is the essential standard behind credit scoring: Its rewards practices that show moderate, responsible utilization of credit after some time, because those propensities are probably going to continue.

The score likewise rebuffs conduct that is not all that responsible, for example, applying for a lot of credit you don't require. Numerous people with high credit scores locates that one of only a handful hardly any detriments for them is the number of credit accounts recorded on their reports. At the point when they go to get their credit scores, they're informed that one reason their score isn't considerably higher is that they have "too many open accounts." Many mistakenly expect they can "fix" this issue by closing accounts. In any case, after you've opened the accounts, you've done the damage. You can't fix it by closing the account. You can, however, make matters more awful.

Myth 2: You Can Increase Your Score by Asking Your Credit Card Company to Lower Your Limits

This one is a minor departure from the possibility that decreasing your accessible credit by one way or another enables your score by making you to appear to be less risky to lenders. By and by, it's missing the goal. Narrowing the difference between the credit you use and the credit you have accessible to you can negatively affect your score. It doesn't make a difference that you requested the decrease; the FICO formula doesn't recognize lower limits that you mentioned and lower limits forced by a creditor. All it sees is less difference between your balances and your limits, and that is not good. If that, you need to enable your score, to handle the issue from the opposite end: by paying down your debt. Expanding the gap between your balance and your credit limit positively affects your score.

Myth 3: You Need to Pay Interest to Obtain a Good Credit Score

This is the precise inverse of the past myth, and it's similarly as misinformed. It is not necessary for you to carry a balance on your credit cards and pay interest to have a good score. As you've perused a few times as of now, your credit reports—and subsequently the FICO formula—make no differentiation between balances you carry month to month and balances that you pay off. Savvy consumers don't carry credit card balances under any circumstances, and not to improve their scores. Presently, the facts confirm that to get the highest FICO scores, you must have both revolving accounts, for example, credit cards, and instalment loans, for example, a mortgage or car loan. What's more, except for those 0 per cent rates used to drive auto deals after Sept. 11, most instalment loans require paying interest.

Yet, here's a news streak: You don't have to have the highest score to get good credit. Any score more than 720 or so will get you the best rates and terms with numerous lenders. A few, particularly auto and home value lenders, save their best bargains for those with scores more than 760. You don't must have an 850, or even 800 score, to get incredible arrangements. In case you're attempting to improve a fair score, a little, reasonable instalment loan can help—if you can get affirmed for it and pay it off on time. However, some way or another, there's no motivation to stray into the red and pay interest.

Myth 4: Your Closed Accounts Should Indicate "Closed by Consumer," Or They Will Hurt Your Score

The hypothesis behind this myth is that lenders will see a closed account on your credit report and, if not educated generally, will accept that a nauseated creditor cut you off because you botched in some way or another. Obviously, as you most likely are aware at this point, numerous lenders never observe your real report. They're simply taking a gander at your credit score, which couldn't care less who closed a credit card. Fair Isaac figures that if a lender closes your account, it's either for dormancy or because you defaulted. If that you defaulted, that will be sufficiently archived in the account's history. If it makes you feel better to contact the bureaus and guarantee that accounts you closed are recorded as "closed by consumer," by all methods do as such. However, it won't make any distinction to your credit score.

Myth 5: Credit Counseling Is Way Worse Than Bankruptcy

Sometimes this is expressed as "credit advising is as awful as bankruptcy" or "credit directing is as terrible as bankruptcy." None of these statements is valid. A bankruptcy recording is the single most noticeably terrible thing you can do to your credit score. On the other hand, the current FICO formula totally ignores any reference to credit guiding that may be on your credit report. Credit guiding is treated as an impartial factor, neither aiding nor hurting your score. Credit guides, if you're inexperienced with the term, have practical experience in arranging lower interest rates and also working out payment plans for debtors that may some way or another file for bankruptcy. Although credit advisors may consolidate the consumer's bills into one monthly payment, they don't give loans—as debt consolidators do—or guarantee to wipe out or settle debts for not exactly the chief amount you owe.

The fact that credit guiding itself won't affect your score doesn't mean, notwithstanding, that enrolling in a credit advisor's debt management plan will leave your credit sound. A few lenders will report you as late only for enrolling in a debt management plan. Their thinking is that you're not paying them what you initially owed, so you ought to need to endure some agony. That is not, by any means, the only way you could be reported late. Not all credit instructors are made equivalent, and some have been blamed for retaining consumer payments that were proposed for creditors.

Chapter 11.

Credit Bureau and Credit Errors

How Do Credit Bureaus Gather the Information?

1. Information supplied by your creditors: Usually, without your consent, your creditors send your credit information to credit bureaus. These records are sent in a format that you don't have to know. But the essential content is the personal information with which you got the loan, the type of loan it is, the terms and conditions, and how well you have played it by the book. Of course, it is not a dark market, so you are expected to know that they send this information to credit bureaus. It is only ironic that these same credit bureaus pay to access the information.

2. Purchased Information: By legal standards, some information isn't accessible to the public. They are considered confidential, not illegal. Due to the legitimacy of credit bureaus, they often access such information, but as you guess, they part with some dough in turn. This sort of information mostly contains public records, judgments, et cetera. You can be sure credit bureaus

are not interested in your personal life, adventures, or such data that are not relevant to your credits, not even your entire finances.

3. Information from other credit bureaus: Despite being competitors, credit bureaus are mandated to share information sometimes. Not all the time, since each one paid to obtain their data. But sensitive data about your credits are exchanged. For example, one updates the others the instant a fraud alert was raised, or attempts were made to hack your credit report et cetera.

There it is! You now understand how consumer reporting agencies gather your data and how it is being used. The next thing we should be talking about is the errors that can be found on your credit report. But before that, you should meet three major credit bureaus. You need to have some idea who you are getting your credit reports from. Right? Entirely logical. Let's latch onto that then.

What Are the Errors That You Should Check Out in Your Credit Report?

1. Personality Identity Information:
Any slack can lead to errors. So, your full name should be spelled and arranged correctly. The same thing about your Social Security Number. How about your address? Your date of birth too. For instance, if you have earlier

raised a fraud alert, security freeze, statement of dispute, et cetera. Whatsoever you have raised earlier, and you find documented, be sure that is exactly what you have here.

2. Credit Account History:

This is the most essential part of the whole credit report as we have earlier disclosed. You may want to pay extra attention to every detail provided here, from the reports of lenders on the transaction you have had with them, to the type of transaction stated that you have had. You also want to check their reports on the agreed duration, the duration you paid, your credit limit, your payment pattern, history, et cetera. Data as simple as account name and number should be doubly verified. I'll be quick to add that a leak is possible from anywhere, your credit union, credit card issuer, or your credit bureau themselves.

3. Credit Inquiries:

Only creditors to whom you apply for a loan can automatically request for your report. The list of the inquirers and the type of credit you're hoping to have with them are displayed here. You want to make sure that a stranger or an unknown company hasn't woken up one day to start gathering data on your credits. The instant you find one such, you have got something to fix on your credit.

Check Out Your Credit Report

4. Public Records:

To cap this, you need to scan through your public records too. We know that bad records don't help anyone, and it can't be exciting to find strange ones in your report. If one of your credit records is overdue for removal, there is no reason you should still have it there. For the records that are still to be reflected, you want to make sure they are not understated or exaggerated. Inconsistency and inaccuracy can give you a bad light in front of every creditor.

There we are! You have just taken a tour of the Credit Bureaus and the errors you may pick out on your credit report. With that last lesson in mind, let's see about fixing your credit reports!

How Can You Get a Free Credit Report?

If you are reading this from any other part of the world, I hate to say you'd have to consult something else. Perhaps your government service, a credit officer, or anything. But if you are wondering how to do it in the US, it is laid on the lines here.

You need to remember that if you are checking a similar site and not exactly this, you may be charged at some point or worst, you might be playing into a fraudster's net. Right after filling the personal data, pick your preferred credit report (whether Equifax, Experian, or Trans union). On the next display, you verify your identity by answering a few questions that are directly related to your credit history. Then, your credit report is displayed on the screen. You can simply print or return to view. Right-on. If not this, consider calling 1-877-322-8228 and go through a similar process over the phone. You'd have to wait for a couple of weeks or one more before receiving your credit report.

Chapter 12.

How Fast and How Many Points Will a Credit Score Improve

Realistic Time Frame for a Noticeable Improvement

As mentioned, there are many steps you can take to improve your credit score. By paying off any credit card debt, disputing any errors in the report, or by even paying off any collection accounts, you can significantly improve your credit score. You must take steps to increase the positive information, reduce the negative impact, or a combination of the two in the credit report. By doing this, you can start seeing an improvement in your credit score within a couple of weeks. For instance, by doing something as simple as making monthly payments on time, you can improve your credit score. It would help if you did this consistently, as it isn't a one-time thing. You can see an improvement in your credit score within weeks, but for a significant change, that will take a couple of months at least. Here are three factors that define the time frame for improving your credit score.

The first factor is the starting point. It takes at least a month to develop your credit score on your own. If you are trying to repair your credit, then it will take longer. For instance, if you are eligible only for a secured credit card and have damaged credit, then it can take anywhere between 12 to 18 months to improve the credit score. The time frame will depend on how responsibly you use the approved card. The amount of pre-existing negative and positive information in your credit report will also influence this time frame.

The second factor relates to the punctuality of your monthly payments. Your credit score depends on the compilation of information in the credit report. To repair damaged credit, you must keep adding positive information to the report every month. It means that you must pay all your bills, including any credit card bills or monthly repayment of a loan on time. If you do this consistently for a couple of months, it will improve your credit rating. Also, if you have a credit card, try not to max it and instead, use it wisely. Maintaining a healthy level of utilization can add positive points to your credit score.

The third factor is to define what improvement means to you. You will start to see your credit rate improving by a few points in a couple of weeks while it takes a couple of months to see your score change from bad to good. So, your perception of what improvement means matters while repairing your damaged credit.

At times, a minor mistake like maxing out the credit card limit or missing a payment can damage your credit. Some might be trying to recover from things they didn't realize could harm their credit like applying for a new credit card or closing an account. Others might be dealing with more significant issues like bankruptcy. Depending on the reason that led to the depreciation of their credit rating, the time taken to get back on track will vary.

You might not have realized it, but whenever you apply for a new line of credit or close an existing account, it reduces your credit rating. The damage in such instances is minor, and the recovery time is around three months. Some major issues severely damage your credit ratings like defaulting on payments and bankruptcy. The average recovery time for bankruptcy is over six years. You can fix the damage from defaulting on a payment within two years. Then there are moderate issues like maxing out the credit card and the recovery time for these issues is three months or more.

These are just examples of how long it can take and isn't a precise estimate. The period of recovery also depends on the other information present on the credit report. Apart from this, the amount of positive and negative information on the credit report influences the recovery time. If you have a solid credit history, then it is easier to fix a misstep. However, if your credit report is riddled with mistakes, it will become quite challenging to repair. The lower your credit score, the lesser ground you have to cover, and the easier it is to improve the score. For instance, A and B have both defaulted on their mortgage payments. A has a credit score of 780, while B's credit score is only 680. A will take anywhere between 3-7 years to repair the score while B can repair it within ten months. Improving your credit score isn't a one-time thing and is a continuous process. The addition of information to the credit report will keep altering the credit score. Your financial goals, along with your existing financial position, are two factors that influence your need to improve the credit score.

What Impacts a Credit Report?

From a lender's perspective, the following points are positive items on a credit report.

- If you pay your bills on time and do so consistently.

- Have been and still can maintain a reasonable balance of unused credit.

- Apply for credit only when the need arises. When you do this, the number of inquiries against you is to a bare minimum.

- Consistently check your annual credit reports and correct any mistakes in them.

- Certain red flags that a potential lender looks for in a borrower's credit report include the following.

As you can see, different factors influence your credit score. Every financial transaction that you make impacts your annual credit report. Paying your monthly cable bill might be a small transaction, but it does affect your credit report. If you consistently pay your monthly utility bills, it will help improve your credit score. However, if you get behind on payments or miss due dates on monthly utility bills, then it will significantly decrease your credit score.

If your credit score is less than 579, then you will be viewed as a risky borrower by the lenders. A score of 582 to 669 might qualify you for approval of loans from some vendors. A good credit score is one, which is between 670 and 739. You are a dependable borrower if your score is higher than 740. You qualify as an exceptional borrower if your credit score is more than 800.

Why No One Can Guarantee an Increase in Points

As mentioned earlier, your credit score is a three-digit number. Not just banks and lenders, but several other companies have also started using credit score as a measure of your ability to repay a debt. Equifax, Trans Union, and Experian are the three main credit bureaus that create all the credit reports. Vantage Score and The Fair Isaac Co-operation (FICO), are credit scoring models which then use the information given in the credit reports for coming up with an individual's credit score. The credit score is usually in the range of 300 to 850.

The credit bureaus might also, at times, generate credit scores based on some other proprietary model. The credit score is calculated based on different things like the frequency of payments, duration of the accounts, or the expenditure you incur and so on. Credit scores aren't influenced by personal demographics like sex, age, religion, nationality, or marital status.

There are different ways in which credit scores are calculated, and therefore, it is not unusual to have multiple scores simultaneously. Your credit scores depend on the bureau or the agencies that specific lender reports. For instance, a lender might report to two agencies. You can have multiple credit scores if a lender doesn't report to all three agencies at the same time. Apart from this, the lending situation can also mean that you have different scores. For instance, the credit model used by a mortgage lender will be different from that used by other lenders.

Regardless of the model used, these scores are based on all the information present in the credit report. However, the formula that is used for obtaining these credit scores is closely guarded much like the fried chicken recipe at KFC or the formula used in Coca-Cola. Certain factors have a positive or negative influence on your credit rating. If you look at all the information that is available online, you will notice that you can certainly improve your credit rating by following specific steps. The one thing that no one guarantees is the number of points that are associated with each factor that influences the credit score.

It is safe to assume that not paying your cable bill for six months will hurt your credit score. However, it isn't possible to estimate the number of points you will lose when you get behind on your payments. This estimation isn't possible because the formula used for calculating the score is safely guarded. Apart from this, the effect that a specific factor has on one's credit score also depends on their existing credit score.

Chapter 13.

Techniques to Rebuild your Credit

Pay off what you owe: While this is going to be easier said than done in most situations, according to Experian, the ideal amount of credit utilization that you want is 30 per cent or less. While there are other ways to increase your credit utilization rating, paying off what you owe on time each month will also go towards showing you can pay your bills on time, essentially pulling double duty when it comes to improving your credit score. It will also make it easier to follow through on the following tips.

Pay your credit card bills twice a month: If you have a credit card that you use on a regular basis, say for example because it offers you reward points, so much so that you max it out each month, it may actually be hurting your credit even though you pay it off in full at the end of each month. This may be the case due to the way the credit card company reports to the credit bureau; depending on when they report each month it could show that your credit utilization rate is close to 100 per cent depending on what your credit line currently is, thus hurting your credit score. As such, paying off your credit card in two smaller chunks throughout the month can actually help boost your credit without costing you anything extra overall.

Increase your credit limit: If you aren't currently able to pay down your credit card balance, you can still improve your credit utilization rate by increasing your current credit limit. This is an easy way to improve your credit utilization rate without putting any more money out up front. If you do this, however, it is important that you don't take advantage of the increased credit line as if you find yourself up against the limit again you will be worse off than when you started. Only pursue this option if you have the willpower to avoid racking up extra charges, especially if you are already strapped when it comes to the payments you need to make each month; decreasing your credit utilization limit while also making more late payments is a lateral move at best.

Open a new account: Improving your credit utilization rate is one of the best ways to start rebuilding your credit. If your current credit card company won't increase your credit limit you may way to try applying for another credit card instead. If your credit is not so hot then your rates are going to be higher, but this won't matter as long as you don't plan on using the card in the first place. Remember, credit utilization rate is a combination of your total available lines of credit so this can be a good way to drop your current utilization rate substantially, especially if you won't be able to pay off what you currently owe for a significant period of time.

Keep in mind, however, that if you choose this route then you are only going to want to apply for one new card every couple of months, especially if you aren't sure if you are going to be approved, as too many hard credit inquiries will only cause your credit score to drop, even if you do end up with a better credit utilization rate as a result. Spreading out these requests will give the inquiries time to drop off naturally and will prevent you from looking desperate to potential lenders which can also make it more difficult to get a new card.

Authorized users: If you don't have the credit to get a new credit card, or even to extend your current credit line, then your best choice may be to find someone you trust and ask them to become an authorized user on their card. While most people will likely balk at the idea, you may be able to pacify them by explaining that you don't need a copy of their card or have any intent on using it, simply being listed on the card is enough to improve your credit utilization rating. Not only that, but you will also get credit for the on-time payments that this other person makes as well.

Make Sure You Can Limit as Much as Possible the Hard Inquiries to Get the Best Results with This

Chapter 14.

Resolving Bad Credit Situation

Most people who are regarded as a bad credit risk is likely to be shut out by the same society, which flourishes on credit. You may find this such a huge contradiction. Being marked as having a bad credit may result in having deep internal wounds. This is because, naturally, you would not want your neighbors to find out about your bad credit. Worse, it would be a dishonor in your part if your entire community would find out and be the topic of their gossips.

In truth, however, you do not have to deal with this type of mentality even if you have a bad credit situation. This issue is only a result of exaggeration from federal authorities and financial institutions that almost 40% to 45% of the people are in a bad credit situation. On the other hand, you need to understand that having a bad credit is not the end of the world. Bad credit only implies that future financial institutions will be careful when carrying out transactions with you. For instance, you may be obliged to pay earlier than you used to, which is to be expected. Besides, if you were in the shoes of these financial institutions, you would also do the same.

Fortunately, there are several enterprises and people who are adept in repairing a bad credit situation. Furthermore, there are books, e-books, videos, DVDs, and cd's that can educate you about various credit situations.

If you are already in a situation of bad credit, it is best to use real money when purchasing instead of plastic, such as credit cards. This can help you spend less, and you will be inclined to avoid even the most effective marketing strategies of companies. You need to get a hold of yourself by learning the techniques and tools on how you can cope with your bad credit situation. The key is to fight the situation in order to restore your good financial state as well as your dignity.

Some Simple Tips on Resolving a Bad Credit Situation

Probably the worst situation that a credit card holder would be in is a bad credit situation. Apart from hindering one's current life, it can also affect the potential of applying for or securing a loan.

There are several factors that may lead to a bad credit situation. The most common of which is overspending. This is considered as the most considerable factor that result in a bad credit situation.

Another factor is the non-payment on time. Often, people, especially credit card holders neglect paying on time for their different purchases, which later affect their credit history.

Inevitable conditions such as unemployment, health problems, and financial setbacks also lead to having a bad credit situation. These are conditions wherein people are left with no choice but to spend without considering their credit scores.

Fortunately, there are various ways to improve your credit score through proper rules, which can help you resolve your situation on time. First, you can check for the consistency of your credit report. This will ensure that no wrong information and mistakes are included in your report. Should there be any inaccuracy, make sure to report it at once to the concerned credit bureau or creditor to carry out the necessary correction.

Second, it is best to keep a budget for your expenses. This involves discerning the items, which added considerably to your bad credit rating. It also involves saving money to repay debts and controlling yourself on overspending.

Third, set an appointment with your creditors and request for a plan through which you can pay your debt appropriately. It is best to consult them in establishing the plan so that you can pay your debt in an effective way.

Fourth, you can ask for counselling from various organizations in order to improve your bad credit rating. These organizations can carry out negotiations with your creditors by convincing the latter to lower the interest rate and create a repayment plan for you.

Fifth, make sure to inform your creditors in advance if you are going to skip a repayment. However, it is best to avoid skipping payments since it would not always be in your favor.

Finally, make sure you are determined to follow the repayment plan that your creditor has provided for you. It is best not to play around with your creditors, especially when they have given you the chance to repay your debt in the most convenient way.

Important Steps to Take Towards Credit Repair

By now, you should already know how credit serves as an important tool in your life. For one, there are many things that having a good credit rating allows you to have. These include being able to rent a house or property, having a credit card, and qualifying for in-store financing among others. When you have a poor credit rating, it is advisable to take the necessary steps for to repair it. However, the process of repairing credit is usually slow and necessitates for rebuilding your credit rating over time. Fortunately, there are some tips that you can follow to start the credit repair process as soon as possible.

One, you can add accounts to your credit report. Then, check for errors or discrepancies. If there are none, this means your credit rating is "poor" because your credit history is insufficient to reflect a good rating and not due to outstanding debts.

There are types of credit that credit bureaus do not tracked. These credit types usually come from small organizations. For instance, department store cards or gas cards are not included in your credit report. If you add these accounts to your credit report, you can rebuild a good credit rating. Thus, you should ask the concerned credit bureau to track these accounts. However, most credit bureaus ask for additional service fee when adding types of credit from small organizations. Only verifiable accounts are usually tracked by credit bureaus and added to your file free of charge.

Two, you can seek the help of a credit counsellor. When you become entangled in debt, it can be difficult to come out of it, especially if it has already fed on itself. This means that your original debt amount has gone higher due to its interest. Furthermore, if you find it taxing to carry out a credit repair on your own or continually encounter problems during the process of credit repair, you should consult a credit counselling agency.

There is a huge difference between a credit counselling company and a credit repair company. Credit counselling companies are non-profit services that offers guidance and advice on how to do a credit repair, while credit repair companies are for-profit organizations that charge fees for taking steps for repairing your credit; however, these steps are not necessarily legal or particularly conscious about ethics.

You can tell if you have found a good credit counsellor when he/she is able to make a realistic budget in which you can stick to as well as help in making practical decisions about your debts.

By adding accounts to your credit report and consulting a credit counsellor as necessary, you can make the process of credit repair easy. Make sure that the account that you will add to your credit report are in good standing.

Keep in mind that it can take a long time to obtain a good credit rating and an extremely short period to destroy it. Once your credit rating is damaged, you need to accept that there is no quick way to repair it. You will be obliged to rebuild your good credit standing from scratch. As such, you need to avoid the promises of credit repair companies that they have quick and easy solutions for a fee. An intelligent and practical way of repairing your credit is to improve your budgeting as well as spending habits.

Conclusion

The fact that you made it here goes a long way to show how serious you are about getting the credit score you desire. However, remember that it is not possible to enhance your credit score overnight. But by following the information in this book and implementing it the right way, you will start to see your credit rating go up.

No one who is starting out in life expects to find themselves in financial turmoil. However, for most people, it will happen at some point during our adult lives. The three-digit FICO score can have a stronger impact on our future than any other grade we get in our lives. Yet, no matter how bad it seems there is no point where it can't be turned around and improved.

The reality is that we live in a society that almost demands that we have some form of credit, not to get ahead, but simply to survive. When we are without it, we suffer in more ways than one.

What better reason is there to start mending our financial health than this? Yes, it can be scary, unpredictable, and stressful but by applying the strategies outlined in this book, you can find your way to a successful credit repair without the additional expense of hiring services to do it for you.

There is an excellent benefit to fixing your credit yourself. Not only do you save yourself from an additional expense when you are already financially strapped, but you become an expert and play a major starring role in your own life.

As you can see, your credit score has a lot more to it than you think. It is one of the most important things to have control of to live a better life. Not only will great credit provide you with a sense of pride, but it will also allow you to do the things and buy the things that you want. We all dream of a certain home or car. Make that dream a reality with good responsible habits.

One of those habits is working on your credit. Now, there are many things that go along with credit when it comes to being successful. Having an excellent credit score will save you a lot of pain and emotional stress. Great credit will get you one step closer to living the life you want to live — a life of financial stability and happiness.

Maybe you are seeking to rebuild your credit score, I have given out some tips needed on how to improve your credit scores, basics of credit repair, how you could repair your credit, the FICO score, and how credit cards could affect your scores. However, you need to take action to get the desired results. If you are in debt or you are struggling with bad credit, the book opens you to ten steps that could be taken as a road towards getting 100 points in 30 days. Pleasure is far from the reason for writing this book. But the book was written to guide, direct, and inspire you in taking the needed actions to improve yourself as an individual. Your success is thus dependent on the practical actions you employ to improve yourself.

I hope this book helps you on your journey to better credit. But my main hope is to help anyone out there who is struggling to achieve greatness. With the power of the mind, anything is possible. Now get out there and increase your credit.

Dave R. W. Graham

BOOK 2: CREDIT REPAIR SECRETS

Learn the Strategies and Techniques of Consultants and Credit Attorneys to Fix your Bad Debt and Improve your Business or Personal Finance. Including Dispute Letters

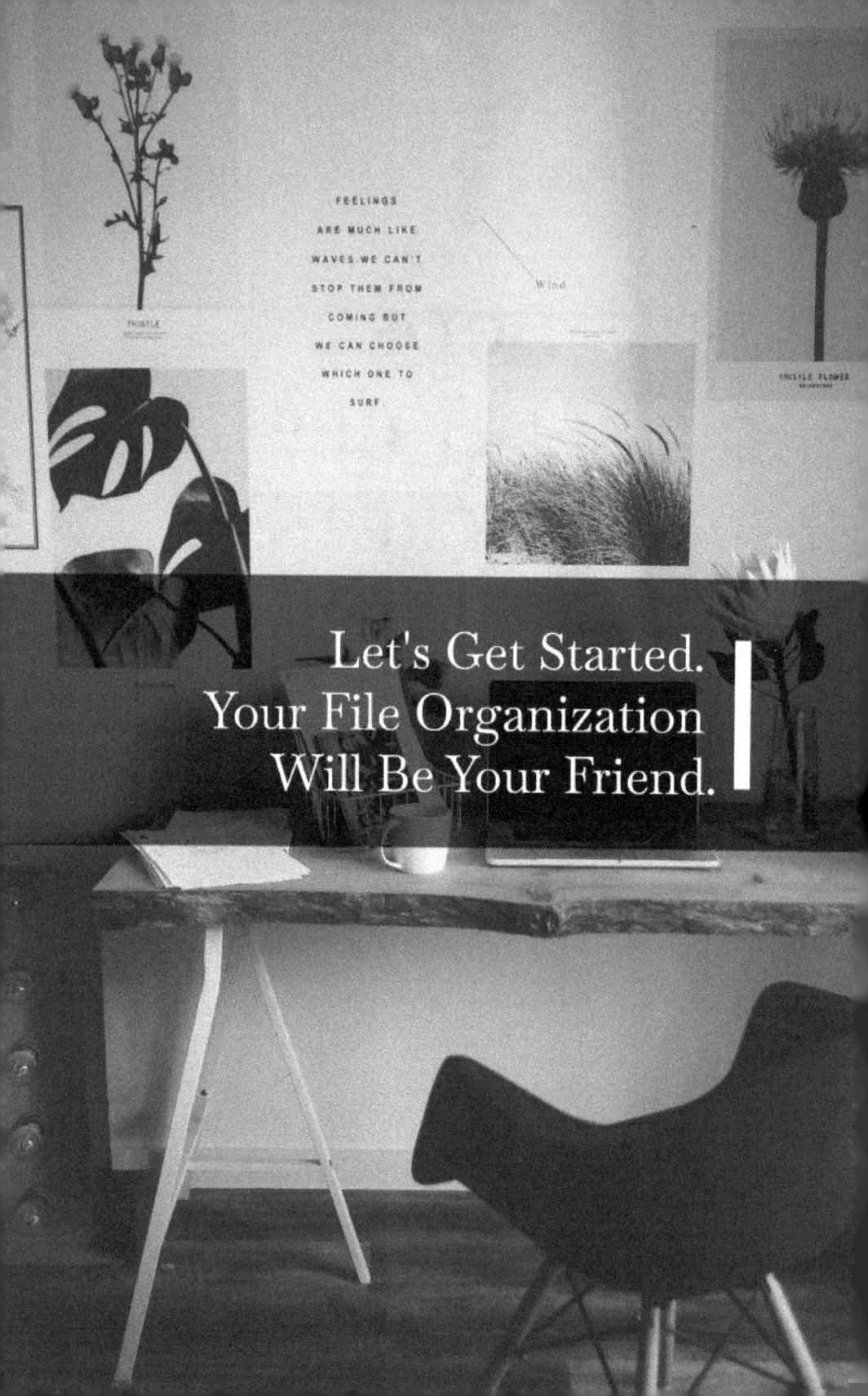

Let's Get Started.
Your File Organization Will Be Your Friend.

Introduction

Credit simply refers to the ability to borrow. We all need money to cater for various expenditures in life. However, just like any other economic resource, it is never enough, which means we are limited to what we can do since almost everything nowadays needs money. Currently where consumer price rises are quite apparent, it is getting tougher and tougher for the average person to afford a lifestyle. Right from consumer products to services, everything is now extremely expensive and people need to arrange for a bagful of money to lead a normal life. But it is not possible for him or her to arrange for this money through their monthly income alone and many have to rely on some external sources of credit. For instance, without additional or external financing, individuals and corporations cannot expand or grow financially.

They must have some money at their disposal to cater for all their monthly/yearly financial needs. Borrowing is one of the most reliable sources of financing there is available but, of course, it comes at a cost. If your credit hasn't improved very much, even though you're sure you've followed all the steps correctly, don't give up on trying to improve your credit. There're several things you can do, which will at least do some sort of damage control. The consequences of the negative items in your credit report will significantly be reduced. It is easy to get discouraged at this point and skip over the damage control step, but keep in mind that you have to put in some effort. The damage control might come in handy in the future, when you try again to repair your credit. All the information you've collected now will be useful in a future credit repair because some of the problems you've encountered now and that you found out are correct might be outdated (over seven years old) soon or your financial situation may improve over time, giving you more grounds for negotiation. Most importantly, by doing a bit of credit repairing and damage control now, this will give you a better starting point for a future credit repair that will be a lot more successful.

The first thing you must do when you've reached this point is to make another list, with the problems you still have and give brief explanations to each. Letters containing no more than one hundred words each, explaining the reason for which you have that negative item on your credit report, will be attached to your credit report, so that when a creditor evaluates your application for a new credit, he will score it correctly and more in your favor. He now knows what's going on in your life and is looking at more than just bad numbers. The letters will be part of your credit report permanently. Each short letter should say the same three things: something bad happened which caused you to default on your payments, but you have remedied that and bounced back and now you are up to date with everything. It should reflect how your financial behavior has improved and a damage control option might even be enough to get you a positive score on a credit application. Just make sure that, if your creditor is reviewing your report in an electronic format, they know that you have included one or more written statements. If he can't find the letters attached, you should have copies to send or hand them to the person working at the creditor's office that oversees your scores.

In this case, I recommend taking legal action. I know what you may be thinking. If you have financial problems, the cost of taking the issue to court will only add to these problems. You don't need a lawyer to take legal action for these issues. You can go to a small claims court with the proof you have gathered and do something about both the creditor and the credit reports agency. This will also entail some research, because the legal procedures involved are quite different from state to state. So, make sure that before you go to court you are prepared and brush up on the legislation in the part of the country you're in. If you have been wronged, it's worth the extra effort, especially since it will turn your credit from bad to good.

Negative Impacts of a Bad Credit Rating

A person with a bad credit score can still obtain credit but may feel the consequences are too much. A poor credit score will result in high-interest rates that can quickly become expensive, especially if you take longer to pay your accounts. A good, excellent, or exceptional credit score will reduce the interest charges and help you to save money in the long run. There are many other benefits to having a good credit score.

Your credit score is one way for the landlord to learn more about prospective tenants. The landlord or rental agency will often use your credit report to see if you pay on time or miss payments. Often, landlords are more willing to let property to people with a high credit score and will out rightly reject applicants with a low credit score. A person with a good credit score is more likely to be approved for renting property since the landlord knows that the person is likely to pay.

Lenders will always choose a customer who has security when it comes to providing credit facilities. Owning an apartment, vehicle, or other assets will give banks the knowledge that you can pay them back. Stable assets help in negotiations with financial institutions for decreasing interest rates and down payments.

A person with a low credit score is perceived to be a high-risk client. The insurance company assumes that these people are more likely to claim from the insurance for unnecessary or fraudulent claims. This lack of trust results in higher insurance premiums.

A similar concept to the credit score is an insurance score used in some companies. The scores are not the same but the general principle of a higher score is better stays the same. Your credit score will greatly influence your insurance score.

Business credit cards offer similar rewards to personal credit cards, but you will only get these if the business has a good credit score. Most of the rewards for business will be in the form of a cash back percentage on the purchases made with the business credit card.

Why You Should Prioritize Credit Repair

It's simple. Credit is your credibility as related to your name and social security number. Your credibility is built from your own financial borrowing patterns. You can develop creditability within any nation, organization, company or with an individual, but being financially credible as we know it here in America comes from our dealings with lenders, banks and other forms of financial institutions. These financial entities furnish our information to credit agencies and companies that import and then summarized our activities into algorithms, which they use to generate credit scores. These credit agencies - also referred to as credit bureaus - are corporations that store our information in a file to identify our past and current creditability but more importantly they determine our future credit worthiness. Your past behavior will dictate your current credit standing or whether you can be trusted to borrow a small sum, pay it back on set terms and if you can, you will then become more credible. It's that simple.

Chapter 1.

How to Get Started

Getting Started Cleaning up Your Credit, The Debt Snowball

Before you can start paying off your debt, it is important to come up with a plan for debt repayment. If you have just one debt to worry about, then the best strategy is to start repaying as much as you can every month. You must keep doing this until you are debt-free.

If you are like a lot of others who are in debt, then you might have multiple debts. You must try to come up with the best repayment strategy which appeals to you and works well for your financial situation.

One method for repaying your debts is known as the debt snowball. You start repaying your debts in ascending order- starting from the smallest amount to the largest one. As you start clearing small loans, it will give you the motivation to keep going. You can start enjoying your small wins as you make your way to being debt-free.

You must start paying the minimum balance due on all your debts. Once you do this, divert all your extra funds toward the debt with the smallest amount. Once you clear this debt, all the money you were spending on this repayment can be diverted towards the small debt on your list. Keep doing this until you paid off all your debts. Regardless of the rates of interest payable, you must start with the smallest sum due and make your way to the largest one. If you ever played in the snow and made a snowball, you will realize that as the snowball rolls on the ground, it keeps collecting more and more snow and becomes bigger. So, every small debt you repay will free up sufficient funds to repay the debt.

Let us assume that you have four debts, and their details are as follows:

- An auto loan repayable at 4.5% for $16,000.
- A student loan repayable at 6.5% for $30,000.
- A personal loan repayable at 8% for $10,000.
- A credit card debt repayable at 21% for $7000.

So, you will start by repaying your credit card debt, which is at $7000. Once you repay this diet and have paid the minimum balance due for all the other loans. All the interest which was payable towards the credit card debt can be successfully redirected toward the payment of the other loans. So, you will start with your credit card debt, then the personal loan, auto loan, and then finally the student loan.

This is a great technique to pay your debts, especially if you have several small debts. At times, it can be rather overwhelming and scary when you look at a major debt. It can also be the reason for losing your motivation.

To avoid this, when you start clearing the small debts, the number of loans you have to repay will reduce. If you have five loans, and you repay two loans, the figure somehow looks more manageable. Instead of worrying about repaying all the five loans at the same time, you can concentrate on repaying the smallest ones, and then be left with only the major debts.

How debt snowball method works:

Step 1: List the debts from lowest to highest.

Stage 2: Make minimum payments on all but the smallest debts

Stage 3: Follow this process with as you clear all your debt. The more you pay off, the more your freed-up money grows it is like a snowball going downhill.

What You Should Include in Your Debt Snowball?

Your debt snowball should include all non-mortgage debt, a loan that is described as anything else you owe to anyone.

- Car notes
- Credit card balances
- Home equity loans
- Medical bills
- Payday loans
- Personal loans
- Student loans

When compared to the Avalanche method, by using the snowball method, you might end up paying more interest in the long run. Since the interest rates are never taken into consideration in this method, any account, which has a higher rate of interest and a large outstanding balance, will be left towards the end. So, the interest payable will obviously increase.

Is Credit Repair Ethical?

Beware, not all credit repair companies are ethical. Do not fall for scams that promise they can take a bad credit record and turn it around overnight. Or that guarantee they can "force" the credit bureaus to remove all negative (but accurate) information from your credit file immediately. It takes time and your cooperation to improve your credit. Trust me when I tell you that a credit repair company cannot push around the large credit bureaus. Never mind order them to do things like immediately remove foreclosures or missed payments from the records of their client's. Inaccurate information can be easily fixed. However, removing accurate negative information takes a plan and is rarely done overnight. That usually requires filing official disputes, and careful negotiations with your creditors.

Some credit repair companies not only misrepresent what they can do for you, but also practice illegal or fraudulent ways of trying to improve your credit. Often, they will reorganize as a non-profit to get around state and federal laws that govern the industry. If you are desperate enough, you may be tempted to risk some of these illegal actions, but we would not recommend it. Also, be wary of credit repair companies that want to be paid up front. People have lost hundreds, and in some cases thousands of dollars to credit repair scams.

The Warning Signs When Choosing a Credit Repair Company
- -They recommend that you do not contact credit bureaus directly.
- -They do not disclose your legal rights or what you can do yourself.
- -They want you to pay upfront based on their verbal promises before they do any work. It is illegal for them to charge you up front. They can only charge you after they have completed the services they contracted for.
- -They suggest unethical or illegal actions such as making false statements on a loan application, misrepresenting your social security number, or obtaining an EIN number under false pretensions. The use of these tactics could constitute general fraud, civil fraud, mail fraud, wire fraud, and get you into a lot of trouble.

Once you receive a copy of your free credit report, take note of your three-digit credit score, and note any damage to your credit standing due to an increased credit utilization, derogatory marks on your report, missed/late payments on your credit cards, closure of old accounts or recent applications for a new credit card/loan. Sometimes, credit repair can be very simple when it involves issues such as fixing disputing mistakes shown on your credit reports with the credit reporting agencies/providers, or an extensive repair, when the issue is about identity theft or fundamental financial issues like budgeting. While you seek to rebuild and repair your credit, you are rectifying a poor credit score, or paying a company to report and remove any incorrect items from your report. Your credit history is vital to understanding your credit standing, and you can file disputes where you observe inaccurate information on your credit report.

What is Credit Repair?

Remember, credit repair entails actions that are taken to rectify inaccuracies in your credit reports, and (re)build an awesome credit history for an improved/higher credit score. The Fair Credit Reporting Act (FCRA) stipulates accurate information of consumers on the credit bureau's files, and it approves consumers' right to dispute questionable information. A poor credit is a credit score below 580, and any credit sore between 580-669 is rated fairly by lenders, even though it is questionable for loan approvals. If your credit score falls in these ranges, due to late student loan payment, collection accounts, foreclosure, or years of increased credit card balance, this will drag your credit score down significantly which will make you unqualified for the approval of a new credit card or loan. Surprisingly, you could take matters into your own hands and repair your credit yourself with a copy of your credit report.

Self-Credit Repair Step

Credit repair is not only about disputing inaccuracies in your report, but it is also about concentrating your present actions in the management of your credit for a positive credit score. To this effect, you should adhere to the following instructions:

1. Know your credit standing by checking your credit report;
2. Be current on your monthly bills;
3. Dispute any error to correct your credit report for a better credit;
4. Know your current credit utilization rate;
5. Create payment reminders;
6. Choose credit responsibly;
7. Spend less based on your purchase by creating a limit;
8. Improve and think about your credit history;
9. Be current about the number of your credit accounts;
10. Ensure you pay your credit card balances;
11. Avoid applications of new loan.

The Truth About CPNs, or Credit Privacy Numbers

So much hype is built up around the magical theory of CPN numbers, some people referred to them as Credit Profile Numbers, or Credit Privacy Numbers, I have even heard people say Celebrity Privacy Numbers. From my understanding CPN numbers aren't anything new and have been around for a long time. The concept is simple, you can use your same name, alter your birthdate by one year and one day, or you can also keep the same birthday, but it is mandatory that you find a new address that has never been associated with your social security number. Ideally the address of a CPN should be from a zip code that your social security number has never been associated with. Once you take this information and apply for a line of credit with a major creditor, this will tri-merge your new number and you will have a brand-new credit file with all 3 major credit bureaus.

Having a CPN number serves best the people who have messed up credit and just want a fresh start because they may not know how or don't want to learn how to fix their own credit. Law Enforcement has been known incorporate this tactic to create new identities for those who are within the constraints of protective custody, or even deep-cover federal agents. For the everyday person, a new number and a new credit file is looked at as a shortcut, most are just too lazy to get started on fixing their own credit as it is easier to start from scratch rather than repairing their own credit. Others may want to be able to utilize multiple identities to carry more debt, defraud creditors or shield themselves from the liability of everyday life.

Chapter 2.

Understanding FCRA and Section 609

A Summary of Your Rights Under the Fair Credit Reporting Act: What Is the Purpose of the Fair Credit Reporting Act? How Does the FCRA Help Consumers?

When you are going about trying to fix your credit, it can often feel as though the deck is stacked against you, however, the truth of the matter is that there are several laws that can help you to even the odds when it comes to dealing with both creditors and credit bureaus.

FCRA: The FCRA does more than just provide you with a free credit report each year, it also regulates the various credit reporting organizations and helps to ensure that the information they gather on you is both accurate and fair. This means that if you see inaccurate information on your credit report, and report it to the relevant agency, they are legally required to look into the matter and resolve it, typically within 30 days. The same applies to agencies or organizations that generally add details to your credit report. Finally, if an organization that reviews your credit report decides to charge your more or declines to do business with you based on what they find in your report, they are legally obligated to let you know why and what report they found the negative information in.

While this won't help you with that lender, if the information is inaccurate you will at least know where to go to clear up the issue. Additionally, if you report an inaccuracy and the credit reporting agency ignores your request you can sue them to recover the damages or a minimum of $2,500. You may also be able to win an additional amount based on punitive damages and legal fees and any other associated costs. You must file legal proceedings within 5 years of when this occurs.

What Is Section 609? Is a 609 Dispute Letter Effective?

The first thing that we need to take a look at here when it comes to our credit scores is what Section 609 is really all about. This is going to be one of the best ways for you to get your credit score up, and outside of a little calling or sending out mail, you will not have to do as much to get it all done. Let's dive in now and see if we can learn a bit more about it.

The FCRA or the Fair Credit Reporting Act, is going to cover a lot of the aspects and the components of credit checking to make sure that it is able to maintain a reasonable amount of privacy and accuracy along the way. This agency is going to list out all the responsibilities that credit reporting companies, and any credit bureaus, will have, and it also includes the rights of the consumer, which will be your rights in this situation. This Act is going to be the part that will govern how everything is going to work to ensure that all parties are treated in a fair manner.

Other issues that are addressed in this act are going to be done in a manner that is the most favorable to the consumer. This Act is going to limit the access that third-parties can have to your file. You personally have to go through and provide your consent before someone is able to go through and look at your credit score, whether it is a potential employer or another institution providing you with funding.

They are not able to get in and just look at it. Keep in mind that if you do not agree for them to take a look at the information, it is going to likely result in you not getting the funding that you want, because there are very few ways that the institution can fairly assess the risk that you pose to them in terms of creditworthiness.

There are several ways that a credit agency can go through and break or violate the FCRA, so this allows the consumer a way to protect themselves if that proves to be something that needs to happen.

Another thing to note about all of this is that the FCRA is going to be divided into sections. And each of these sections is going to come with a unique set of rules that all credit bureaus need to follow. In particular, section 609 of the FCRA is going to deal with disclosure and is going to put all the burdens of providing the right kind of documentation on the credit bureaus.

This may sound a little bit confusing, but it means that you may have debt or another negative item that is on your credit report, but there is a way to get around this without having to wait for years to get that to drop off your report or having to pay back a debt that you are not able to afford.

Keep in mind that this is not meant to be a method for you to take on a lot of debts that you can't afford and then just dump them. But on occasion, there could be a few that you are able to fight and get an instant boost to your credit score in the process.

You do not have to come up with a way of proving if the item on the credit report is legitimate or not. Instead, that is up to the credit bureaus. And there are many cases where they are not able to do this. Whether they bought the debt and did not have the proper documentation, or there is something else that is wrong with it, the credit company may not be able to prove that you are the owner of it or that you owe on it at all. If this is the case, they have to remove the information from your credit report. When a bad debt is taken off, or even a collection is taken off, that does nothing but a lot of good for your overall score.

Some of Your Rights Under Section 609 and How You Can Use These to Your Advantage. How to Correctly Dispute Errors on Your Credit Report.

According to Section 609 of the Fair Credit Reporting Act, the credit bureaus are not allowed to list any credit agreements without verifying their validity first. The creditor is supposed to send a copy of the credit agreement for the bureaus to validate and keep in case there are any inquiries.

This is important because the bureaus generally skip this step. It is expensive and time consuming for them to verify all the information they receive. By law, the bureaus are required to provide proof that they have verified the information within thirty days. If they cannot provide proof of the original agreement or subsequent evidence of negative listings, and you can prove your identity, then they must remove the listing. It does not matter if the information is accurate or not. That is why it's important to monitor your credit.

To take advantage of this law, the first thing you need to do is to send a physical letter to the billing inquiries address that the creditor provides. If they turn down your request you are then allowed to ask for all the documentation saying why they turned you down.

A subset of this law is what is known as the Hidden Gem Law, this means you can dispute any transaction made within 100 miles of your home, or anywhere in your home state, which exceeds $50. As long as you make a good faith effort to dispute the transaction, and return the item or stop using the service, then the company will likely refund the transaction.

If the debt collector breaks these rules or acts in other ways they are not allowed then you can file a private lawsuit and be recouped costs, fees and damages. What's more, you don't even need to prove damages and you will likely be awarded a minimum of $1,000.

Ways to Approach the Financial Institution

If the credit reporting agency is struggling to alter your report and you think the information is incomplete or wrong --you will want to take action. Below are a few suggestions that will assist you with your attempts.

Contact the Creditor Directly

Contacts the lender, which supplied the advice and demand it inform the credit. Request to Creditor composes your letter or to Eliminate. You can use inaccurate Information. You receive a letter from the lender and ought to be deleted from the credit history if, send a copy of the letter to the bureau that made the faulty report. If you contacted the Funding, it does not need to manage this dispute unless you supply the info. But since you think you also demonstrate a foundation for the belief, and the dispute wasn't properly researched should you increase your complaint, just like the president or CEO, the provider is very likely to reply. If the company cannot or won't help you in removing the info that is inaccurate, call the credit reporting agency.

Document another Dispute with the Credit Reporting Agency with More Information

If you have info backs up your claim, it is possible to submit a fresh dispute. Make sure to provide info. Should you dispute the mistake without giving any info to the bureau, it will determine that your dispute is frivolous, so the bureau does not need to inquire into the issue.

File a Complaint about the Credit Reporting Agency

You can file a complaint regarding a Credit reporting bureau together with the Consumer Financial Protection Bureau (CFPB). The CFPB attempt to have a response and will forward your complaint. In the event the CFPB believes another government agency will be able to assist you, it allows you to know and will forward your complaint.

File a Complaint Concerning the Creditor

If the lender supplied The erroneous or incomplete data fails to revise it or notify the credit reporting service of a correction (or even if it advises the credit reporting bureau of this alteration, but reports the incorrect information again after), you might file a complaint with the Federal Trade Commission (FTC). Or, if the lender is a big institution, you might file a complaint. The CFPB manages Types of agencies, and that means a complaint can document. If you are not sure which agency to contact, begin with CFPB or even the FTC, which will forward your complaint. Normally, you won't be represented by these government agencies. However, they could send an inquiry, and they may take action when there are complaints or proof of wrongdoing.

Complain for Your State Consumer Protection Agency

Some countries have to credit reporting lenders or bureaus furnishing information. File a complaint with the attorney general or consumer protection bureau of your state.

Consider Adding an Explanatory Statement for Your Credit Report

You've got the right Statement to your credit score. As soon as you submit a statement regarding the dispute using a credit reporting agency, the agency must include your statement--or a list of it. It might limit your announcement. In case the agency helps you in writing the excuse. There is not a term limit. Nonetheless, it is a fantastic idea to maintain the announcement shortly. In this way, the credit reporting agency is inclined to utilize your remark.

Chapter 3.

How to Remove Hard Inquiries from Your Credit Report

What Is a Hard Inquiry? Should You Remove Hard Inquiries?

All hard inquiries show up on your credit report and account for about 10% of your total credit score according to the FICO model. If you pull up your own credit report, it is a soft inquiry. If any lender or a creditor checks your credit report to pre-approve you for any existing, of course, it is also soft inquiry. All soft inquiries are exempt from your credit report, and it won't influence your credit score.

Your credit report and credit score will be checked by a potential lender whenever you apply for a loan, credit card, or any other similar credit. However, the lender will do so only after obtaining your approval for the same. Once the lender has your approval, he can approach the credit bureau and request your credit report. Since this inquiry is primarily made to ensure your creditworthiness, it will show up in the credit report.

Now, let us look at why hard inquiries matter and the way they affect your credit report. If your credit report is riddled with multiple hard inquiries made within a short period, it is a red flag for all potential lenders. Multiple hard inquiries show that you are trying to open multiple new accounts. This, in turn, implies that you are in dire need of funds and that your financial position is shaky. It might also be a sign of poor budgeting and the inability to manage your finances. So, it paints a rather negative image in the minds of potential lenders or creditors.

At times, people do make multiple inquiries because they are shopping for the best deal available in the market. Credit rating models are reasonable, and they do consider this possibility. For instance, if you're looking for a mortgage and have made several hard inquiries within 30 days, then all this will be treated as a single hard inquiry. Multiple inquiries will be pardoned provided they are all related to a specific type of credit and are made within a short period. Usually, you will not be denied loans because of the number of hard inquiries on your credit report. A hard inquiry is one of the many factors taken into consideration while determining your creditworthiness. Such inquiries tend to appear on your report for two years. As time passes by, their effect on your credit score reduces. You won't be disqualified for credit by a lender merely because of the hard inquiries. After all, it accounts for only 10% of your total credit score.

If you notice that a hard inquiry on your report is inaccurate, you can raise a dispute about the same and get it removed. If a specific hard inquiry was made without your permission, then it is erroneous. Also, if you notice any hard inquiries made by any unfamiliar lenders in your credit report, please look into it. It can be a sign of identity theft. Carefully go through your credit report and check the accuracy of all the entries reported on it. If any inaccurate hard inquiries are removed from your report, it can help improve your credit score.

If a hard inquiry was made without your authorization or prior approval, then you can get it removed from your credit report along with your credit history. You can do this only when you had no prior knowledge about the hard inquiries. You can also get any other inquiries removed from the credit report, which were made because you were pressurized into accepting an application process even when you weren't interested. Here are a couple of hard inquiries that can be easily disputed and removed from your credit report.

- Any such inquiries that were made without your authorization or consent.
- Any inquiries made without your prior knowledge.
- Any inquiry wherein you were pressurized to accept such an inquiry.
- When the number of inquiries present on the credit report clearly exceed the ones you made.

If you notice any inaccurate hard inquiries on the credit report, send a letter contacting the appropriate credit bureau for its removal. Send the same letter to the concerned lender as well. Only use certified mail for sending both these letters. A certified mail will keep a record of not just the delivery but the receipt of the concerned letter too. You can hold onto this record as legal proof, and it will come in handy if the receiver denies the acceptance of the letter.

Before you send a notice for the removal of a credit inquiry, you must notify the lender. Before you take any legal action, you must notify the concerned parties. At times, the lender might not be as responsive to your request as the credit bureau. I suggest that you don't give up and get any wrong entries removed from your credit report at the earliest. While sending a letter for the removal of the discrepancy, don't forget to attach a copy of your credit report along with it.

If you make multiple hard inquiries within a short period, it is usually considered to be an indication of filing for bankruptcy. It shows that you are running out of funds or have already exhausted the resources available. Apart from this, it makes your financial position seem highly unstable and makes you look like a flight risk for all potential creditors. If you look into multiple sources of credit at the same time for various reasons, it indicates bankruptcy. So, start being mindful of all the hard inquiries you make.

Dispute Flowchart

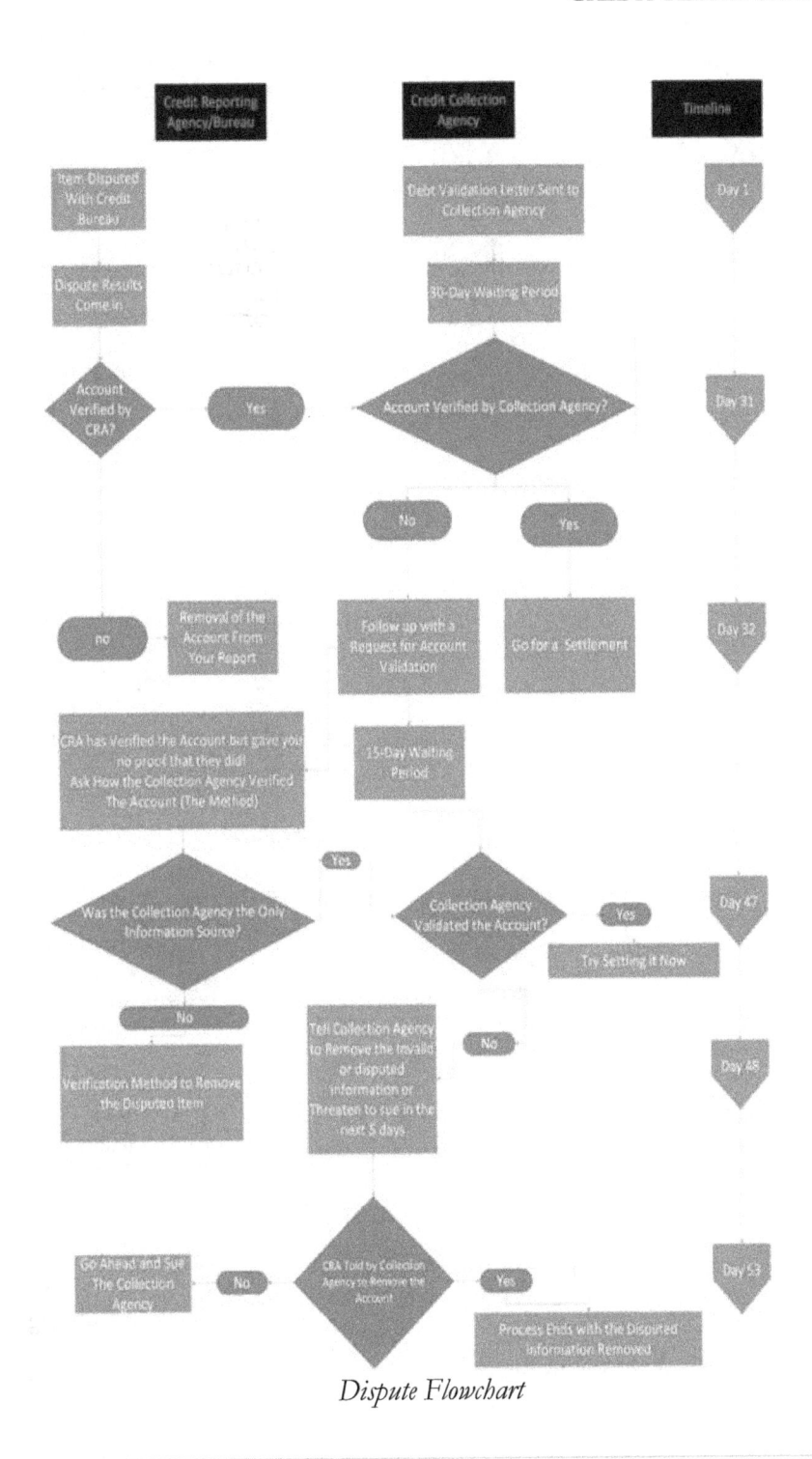

Disputing Inaccurate Hard Inquiries Yourself

The FCRA's regulations state that both the credit bureau (credit reporting company) and the information provider are responsible to correct inaccuracies and fill out incomplete information correctly in your credit report. The information provider is the person, company or organization that provides information about you to the credit reporting company, and may include banks, healthcare providers, grocery stores, clothes shops, landlords, etc.

You have certain rights under FCRA as well.

These include:

- The right to receive a copy of your credit report. This copy should include all updated information from your file at the time of your request.

- A company that denied your request for credit must inform you of the name and address of the credit reporting agency that they contacted. This is only in case that the company denied the application based on the information that the credit reporting company provided.

- If you are unsure of the completeness and accuracy of the information in your credit report and you want to challenge it, you should file a dispute with the credit bureau and the company that gave them the information. Both credit bureau and the information provider are bound by law to investigate the dispute you file.

- If someone received your credit report in the last year for most reasons, or in the last two years for employment reasons, you have every right to know their name.
- You have every right to add a summary explanation if you're not satisfied with the resolution of your dispute.

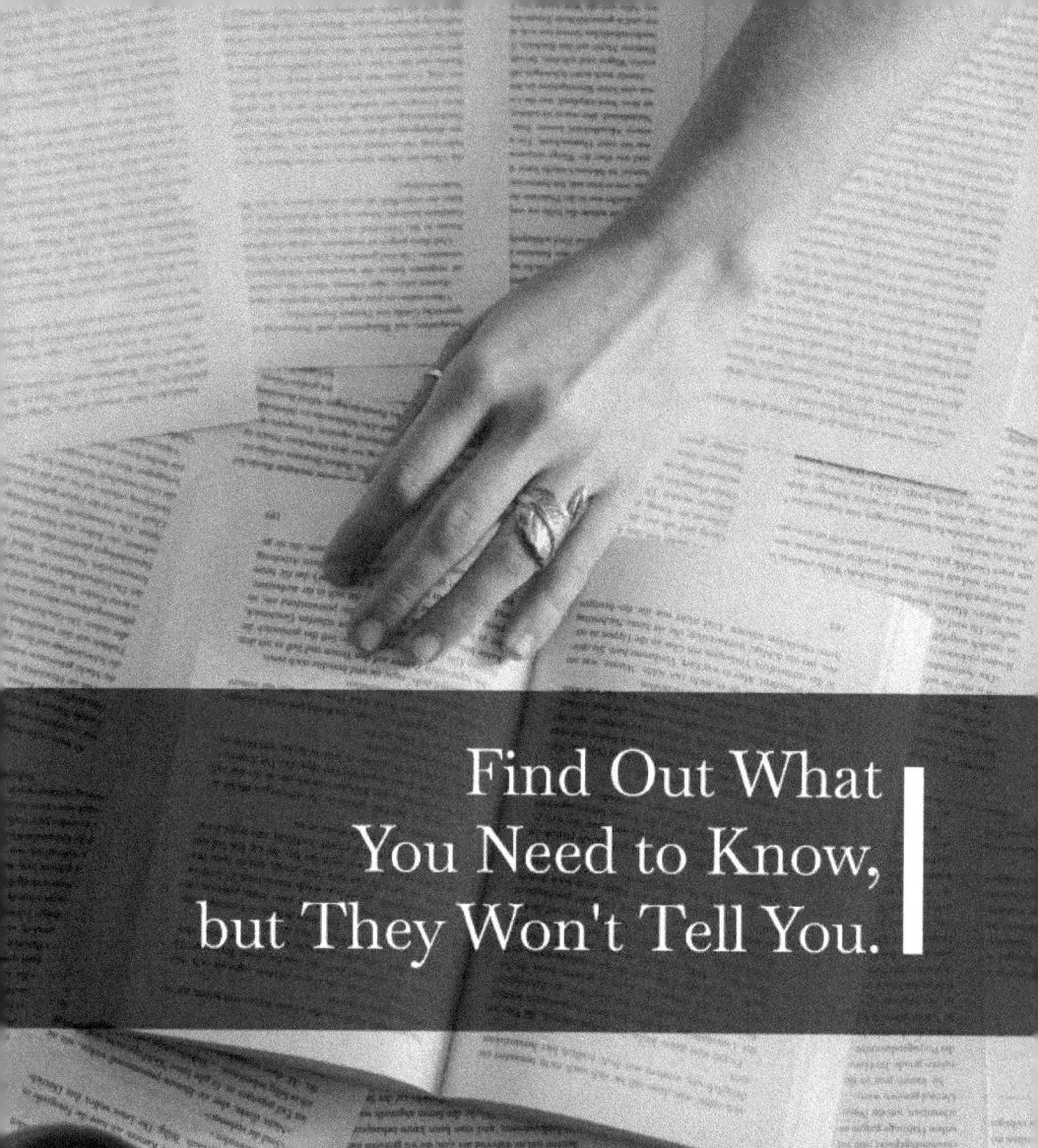

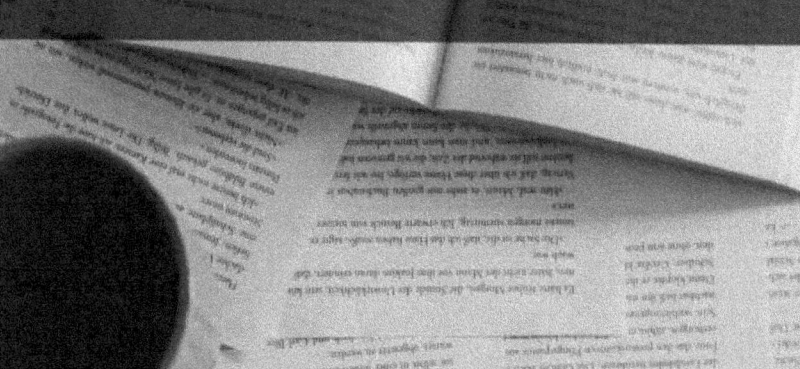

Find Out What You Need to Know, but They Won't Tell You.

Chapter 4.

What the Credit Bureaus and the Lawyers Do Not Want You to Know

How to Deal with the Big Three Credit Bureaus. Who Are, How to Work

In the United States, there are three major credit bureaus: Trans Union, Experian and Equifax. Each of these companies is responsible for collecting information about all consumers' including personal information, habits for paying bills and other financial data to form credit reports. Your credit report, therefore, is unique to you because your spending habits, credit cards, loans and more will differ from other consumers. Furthermore, each credit reporting agency will have a unique formula for calculating your credit score. The information will be similar, but there can be some slight differences.

Credit bureaus are privately held, billion-dollar organizations whose primary reason for existing is to make cash; that is what revenue driven organizations do right? They keep data that lenders furnish them - regardless of whether accurate or inaccurate - about our credit association with them and sell it.

Basic, right? This straightforward plan of action generates over $4 Billion per year!

One wellspring of income for them originates from selling the information on our credit reports to different lenders, managers, insurance agencies, credit card organizations - and whoever else you approve to see your credit information. In addition to the fact that they provide them with crude data; yet they likewise sell them various methods for examining the data to decide the risk of stretching out credit to us. In addition to trading our information to lenders, they likewise sell our information to us - credit scores, credit observing administrations, extortion security, wholesale fraud prevention - interestingly enough this region has quickly gotten perhaps the greatest wellspring of income. Furthermore, those pre-endorsed offers in our letter drop each week; or garbage mail? That's right; they got our information from the credit bureaus as well. Organizations buy in to an assistance provided by the three credit bureaus that sell them a rundown of consumer's credit information that fit a pre-decided criterion.

Today, credit bureaus consistently accumulate information from creditors (banks; credit-card guarantors; mortgage organizations, which have practical experience in loaning cash to home buyers; and different businesses that stretch out credit to people and businesses) and amass it into files on singular consumers and businesses, while refreshing their current files. Information usually remains on a credit report for seven years before being evacuated.

Every one of these three organizations assembles and appropriates information separately, and credit scores and reports vary somewhat from bureau to bureau. Each organization keeps up around 200 million singular consumer credit files. Frequently a lender will utilize an average of the credit evaluations provided by the three unique bureaus when choosing whether or not to make a loan.

Credit bureaus collect information from various sources in accordance with consumer information. The activity is done for various reasons and includes data from singular consumers. Included is the information concerning a people charge payments and their getting. Utilized for evaluating creditworthiness, the information provides lenders with an outline of your accounts if a loan repayment is required. The interest rates charged on a loan are additionally worked out concerning the kind of credit score shown by your experience. It is thusly not a uniform procedure, and your credit report is the significant instrument that affects future loans.

Based on risk based valuing, it pegs various risks on the various customers in this manner deciding the cost you will acquire as a borrower. Done as credit rating, it is an assistance provided to various interested parties in the public. Terrible credit histories are affected for the most part by settled court commitments which mark you for high interest rates every year. Duty liens and bankruptcies, for example, shut you out of the conventional credit lines and may require a great deal of arrangement for any loan to be offered by the bank.

Bureaus collect and examine credit information including financial data, personal information, and elective data. This is given by various sources generally marked data furnishers. These have an exceptional association with the credit bureaus. An average gathering of data furnishers would comprise of creditors, lenders, utilities, and debt collection agencies. Pretty much any association which has had payment involvement in the consumer is qualified including courts. Any data collected for this situation is provided to the credit bureaus for grouping. When it is accumulated, the data is placed into specific repositories and files claimed by the bureau. The information is made accessible to customers upon request. The idea of such information is important to lenders and managers.

The information is in this manner material in various conditions; credit evaluation and business thought are simply part of these. The consumer may likewise require the information to check their individual score and the home proprietor may need to check their inhabitants report before renting an apartment. Since the market is saturated by borrowers, the scores will, in general, be robotic. Straightforward examination would deal with this by giving the client a calculation for speedy appraisal. Checking your score once every other year should deal with errors in your report.

Individuals from the public are qualified for one free credit report from every one of the significant bureaus. This is organized in the Fair Credit Report Act, FCTA. Other government rules associated with the assurance of the consumer incorporate Fair and Accurate Credit Transaction Act, Fair Credit Billing Act and Regulation B. Statutory bodies have additionally been made for the regulation of the credit bureaus. The Fair-Trade Commission serves to as a controller for the consumer credit report agencies while the Office of the Comptroller of Currency fills in as a manager of all banks going about as furnishers.

Chapter 5.

Advice Nobody Tell You

Advice on Right Mind-set for Credit Management

Many folks suffer a financial crisis at some point. They may have to deal with overspending, loss of a job, a family member or personal illness. These financial problems can be and usually are, overwhelming. To make these situations worse, most people don't even know where to begin to solve these financial dilemmas. Our goal here is to shine some light on the strategies to help get youth Accumulating basic consumer debt will chain you into slavery and you could possibly spend your life held down by your own obligations to repay these loans.

What type of credit should you get? That depends on what you plan to do with the money. The most used types of credit are secured and signature credits. For smaller loans, there's no need for that, as no institution would like to end up with a store of household items, so they lend you money or issue a credit card in your name simply based on the strength of your credit so far.

There is hope; you as the borrower have many options to get rid of debt. You can take advantage of budgeting and other techniques, such as debt consolidation, debt settlement, credit counselling and bankruptcy procedures. You just have to choose the best strategy that will work for you. When choosing from the various options, you have to consider your debt level, your discipline and plans for the future.

Advice on How to Manage Bankruptcy and How it Will Affect Credit

Whether you struggle with debt, are unable to meet all your payments on time, have missed multiple payments on your mortgage or car loan, have maxed out your credit cards, are balancing payments on several credit cards to try to keep up to date, or are slipping back on a lot of unsecured debt, the effective bankruptcy option may be what you need to offset your income and debt. If you think the worst possible thing for your credit is bankruptcy, think again. If you're already behind on payments and keep falling further behind or have accounts in collection, bankruptcy may help you start building a strong credit history sooner rather than later.

Before considering how bankruptcy will work for you, you must first familiarize yourself with the various types of bankruptcy, grasp what bankruptcy can and cannot do, and know how it will affect your reputation.

Bankruptcy is a powerful tool for removing or rising most unsecured debts, and can even cut down on most secured debts— giving you a fresh start. But it will live up to 10 years on your credit report (longer if you apply for a $150,000 or more loan), which is longer than almost any other derogatory thing in your history.

Even though a bankruptcy will lower your credit score immediately, the impact may be smaller than you think. "Someone who had spotless credit and a very good FICO score might expect a huge decrease in their ratings, according to Fair Isaac. On the other hand, someone with more derogatory things already reported at their credit report could only see a small decrease in their ratings. "Fair Isaac also warns that the greater the effect on your ranking, the more accounts included in the bankruptcy filing.

Ironically, a bankruptcy will help you start building good credit faster than if you don't file for bankruptcy and keep struggling with more debt than you can afford, particularly if you end up filing bankruptcy again later. Eliminating or eliminating loans by bankruptcy would help you (when the bankruptcy is over) accomplish the two most important goals for a good credit score: meeting your payments on time (35% of your FICO score) and not using the bulk of your available credit (30% of your FICO score). Creditors differ in the way they can offer credit or good interest rates and repayment conditions shortly after a bankruptcy, but they tend to treat the most recent credit issues as more relevant than older problems.

Check Your Credit Report Regularly

When you monitor your credit, you will be able to tell when your report changes. Things to keep an eye on could include your payment history and changes in account balance, among other things.

There are many apps and sites like Credit Sesame and Credit Karma which help you monitor credit for free and will inform you anytime there is a change, to ensure you know what is going on with your credit.

There are tons of tricks and tips you can utilize in maintaining and even improving your credit score. A few of the top steps you can take include not overspending, making payments on time, and paying consistently. All of these will ensure you don't reduce the credit score you battled so hard to build.

How to Negotiate and Settle Large Debt

Knowing which revolving debts to pay off first matters. I will cover 2 different approaches. Which you choose will depend on your need and how well you know yourself.

The first approach I call the Snow Ball method. This is the approach I use personally because I know I need to see results quickly or I will lose interest.

Here's how it works...

Any extra income you have is used to pay down this balance first. Once the card is paid off, then take that same money you were using to pay the first card off and use it to pay down the second card. This works because you have larger and larger sums of money to knock your debt down.

From a psychological point of view, it's very rewarding to see cards with zero balances accumulating as well as having larger and larger sums of money to drive your next balance down. While extremely effective, the Snow Ball method is not the best method for improving your FICO scores.

Most people assume that paying down the card with the highest interest rate would be the next logical step, but that's incorrect. You need to think like FICO and understand what FICO considers important.

When calculating your credit scores, FICO takes four criteria into consideration:

- Overall combined utilization
- Line item utilization
- Number of accounts with a balance

- Number of highly utilized credit cards

Utilization just means how much of your credit you're using. Take out your spread sheet again. First, you'll want to pay off any cards that have low balances on them. Remember that using too many cards is not a good thing, so always keep at least one card at zero.

Next, you'll list your lenders in order of highest utilization to lowest.

For example:

Your Pay-off Priority List should look like this:

- Citibank
- US Bank
- Macy's
- Shell
- Sears

Citibank is first because the amount owed is small... and having a credit card account with a zero balance will increase your score. The other revolving credit cards' order was based on the utilization percentage of each card. This is how you hack FICO's scoring formula to optimize your credit scores.

You will start to see a credit score increase in about 30-40 days. Lenders only update their records with the credit bureaus once a month. The date they update is normally about 10 days after your due date. It's important to note that using your credit cards while you're paying them down is counterproductive.

Chapter 6.

Your Financial Freedom

Financial freedom is a concept that people love to think about but rarely feel like they can reach.

What Is Meant by Financial Freedom?

Financial freedom has no set definition. However, it typically means that you are living comfortably and saving for retirement and in general. It can also mean that you have an emergency reserve set up. In general, financial freedom can mean whatever you want it to mean for you. For example, a prior college student may not think that financial freedom includes paying off all their student loans. This is because, at least currently, a college student who needs to pay their own way realizes they will always be paying off their student loans. However, they might feel that student loans are the only debt they should have. Therefore, being able to pay off credit cards or medical bills leads them to financial freedom.

Some people might feel that financial freedom indicates they have absolutely no debt or loans. This includes them having paid off their mortgage and any car loans. They might also feel that in order to reach financial freedom, they need to be investing in a CD, bond, or even in the stock market.

Other people may feel that financial freedom means they are no longer tied down to a job. They are able to live off their savings or a passive income, and they are able to retire and enjoy life through traveling.

Credit Cards and Financial Freedom - Is It Safe?

One of the biggest questions people have when it comes to financial freedom is whether they can have any credit card accounts in their name. While you may not owe anything on your credit cards (in fact, you might only owe one which you pay off in full every month), is this still financial freedom? In general, this is completely determined by your definition of financial freedom. However, if you ever find yourself not being able to pay off your credit card every month, this is not financial freedom. In most cases, financial freedom does mean you no longer have any debt, or at least that you are free from unnecessary debt, such as credit cards.

Most people are quick to state that financial freedom and credit cards do not go together simply because they are not safe with each other. This is since it is often easy to fall back into thinking you can pay the amount off everything each month and then you become unable to do so. In general, people who reach financial freedom feel that credit cards allow for more of a trap and keep them from ever reaching financial freedom.

However, other people who feel they have reached financial freedom state that as long as you can manage your credit cards wisely, they can be included with your freedom. Some of them also advise that you set up a financial freedom plan. Within this plan, you will state your conditions of using a credit card. Of course, you need to be self-disciplined enough to follow your condition.

The Best Habits to Help You Reach and Protect Your Financial Freedom

When it comes to financial freedom, there are dozens of habits and tips that people provide to help you reach your financial freedom. It is important to note that because financial freedom can vary depending on the person's definition, some of the tips and habits might work for you while others may not. You need to find the ones that work best for you, not the ones that other people say are the best. Therefore, I am going to give you a fairly large list as I want you to make sure that you can find some of the best habits and tips so you can not only reach financial freedom but also protect it.

1. Make a Budget

Making and keeping a budget is one of the first steps everyone should take while heading towards your financial freedom. Even though you might find yourself changing your budget now and then, as you will add or delete bills or receive a different income, you always want to follow it. Not only will this help you in reaching your financial freedom, but continuing to follow your budget will also protect your financial freedom.

Furthermore, creating a monthly budget can make sure that all your bills are being paid and you know exactly where your money is going. For example, you will be able to see how much money you spend on groceries, gas, and eating out at restaurants. This will help you know where you can decrease your spending, which will allow you to save more. There are a lot of great benefits when it comes to creating and sticking with a household budget.

2. Set Up Automatic Savings Account

If you work for an organization that will automatically place a certain percentage of your check into a savings account, take advantage of this. It gives you the idea that you never had the money to begin with, which means you don't plan for it and you won't find yourself taking the money out of savings unless you need it for an emergency. Furthermore, you can set up a separate savings account where this money will go. You can make it so you rarely see this account, however, you want to make sure that your money is deposited and everything looks right on your account. But, the point of this account if you do not touch it, even if you have an emergency. Instead, you will set up a different account for emergency basis.

The other idea to this is you pay yourself first. This is often something that people don't think about because they are more worried about paying off their debt. However, many financial advisors say that you are always number one when it comes to your finances. While you want to pay your bills, you also need to make sure that you and your family are taken care of.

3. Keep Your Credit in Mind Without Obsessing Over It

Your credit score is important, but it is not the most important thing in the world. People often fall into the trap of becoming obsessed over their credit score, especially when they are trying to improve it. One factor to remember is that your credit score is typically only updated every so often. Therefore, you can decide to set time aside every quarter to check on your credit report. When you do this, you not only want to check your score, but you also want to check what the credit bureaus are reporting. Just like you want to make sure everything is correct on your bank account, you want to do the same thing for your credit report.

4. It Is Fine to Live Below Your Means

One of the biggest factors of financial freedom and being able to maintain it is you can make your bills and comfortably live throughout the month. In order to do this, you need to make sure that the money coming into your home is more than the money going out. In other words, you want to live below your means.

This is often difficult for a lot of people because they want to have what other people have. They want to have the newer vehicles, the bigger boat, the newest grill, or anything else. People like to have what their friends and neighbors have. However, one-factor people don't think about is that their friends and neighbors probably don't have financial freedom. Therefore, you want to take a moment to think about what is more important for you. Would you rather be in debt like your friends or you would rather have financial freedom?

5. Speak With a Financial Advisor

Sometimes the best steps we can take when we are working towards financial freedom is to talk with a financial advisor. They can often give up information and help us with a budget, ways to make sure that we get the most out of our income, and also tell us where we might be spending more money than we should. Furthermore, they can help you figure out what the best investments are, which are always helpful when you are looking at financial freedom. At the same time, they can help you plan for your retirement, which is one of the biggest ways you will be able to remain financially free.

6. Completely Pay Off Your Credit Cards

If you are high-interest credit cards, which is often the case, you want to make sure that you pay these off every month. Therefore, your credit card spending should become part of your budget. What this means is you don't want to use your credit card for whatever you feel like. Instead, you want to create a list on when you can and when you can't use your credit card. For example, you might agree that it is fine in emergency situations or during Christmas shopping. You might also feel that you can use it during tips because it has trip insurance attached to it. Whatever you decide, you want to make sure you follow.

You also want to make sure that you pay off any high-interest loans. When it comes to loans that are lower in interest, they won't affect you too much.

7. Track Your Spending

Along with making sure you follow your budget, you also want to track your spending. There are several reasons for this. First, it will help you make sure that your budget is on track. We often forget about automatic bills that are paid monthly or don't realize how much we really spend every month. These factors can make our budget off, which can cause an obstacle when you are working to reaching and keeping your financial freedom.

Fortunately, there are a lot of apps that you can download, many of them are free, which will allow you to track your spending easily. Some of these apps include Mint or Personal Capital. These apps typically give you all the information you need and will automatically tell you how much you are spending and how much income you still hold at the end of the month. Most of these apps will also give you charts to help you see your spending habits in a different way.

Remember The Best Habits to Reach Your Financial Freedom

Chapter 7.

Little Known Facts About Credit

Credit Cards Secrets Revealed

The first step when applying for a credit card is knowing the actual purpose why you are choosing to apply for a credit card in the first place. Some people find credit cards with cash reward to be very attractive. While other people may want to apply for a credit card offering a 12 to 18-month intro of 0% interest rate, so they can make purchases without paying interest for a specific time and take advantage of balance transfers. There are many more reasons why consumers apply for credit cards, but it is important to know the ins and outs about credit card so you can make well-informed decisions.

One of the most important things a consumer should know before applying for a credit card is their credit score. Understanding what your credit score is can put you in the driver's seat when you are determining which is the best credit card for you. Consumers with excellent credit usually qualify for the best offers, but having average to poor credit often means a consumer will pay higher interest rates and possibly hefty annual fees.

Understanding Interest Rates

So, you recently applied for a credit card offering 0% for 6months, fast forward two weeks later you checked your mail and there it is your brand-new credit card with a $5000 limit. You are thrilled because you were planning on using the credit card to book a trip to Cancun and pay off the card over the next five months. So you wasted no time to book your ticket and hotel room; you also purchased things you think are necessary for your trips such as new clothes and shoes. Before long your credit card balance jumped up to $4,500, but not to worry about now because you are planning on paying off your debt before the six-month intro zero per cent grace period expires. Unfortunately, you were not able to pay off your credit card before the six-month interest grace period. To make matters worse, you were only making a minimum payment of approximately $105 every month. But six months later your minimum payments were being applied to the interest and principal on your credit card balance, instead of being applied to just the principal balance. Therefore, if you were to keep making the minimum payment of $105 it would have taken you 56 months to pay off the credit card. You would have also paid approximately $1,280 in interest payments.

Annual Percentage Rate

When you initially applied for a credit card your annual percentage rate (APR) was 11.24%. However, what does this all mean to you? The APR is the annual cost of borrowing money from your credit card. The APR specifically applies to the interest rate that will be charged, if your credit card balance is not paid in full on or before the due date.

Types of APR

There are usually several types of APR that applies to your credit card account. For example, there is an APR for purchases. There is an APR for cash advance, balance transfers; there is an APR that usually goes into effect when you make a late payment or if you violate any other terms of your credit card agreement.

Can My Credit Card Rate Increase?

Your credit card rate can increase if a promotional rate has expired, your credit card rate can increase when you don't follow your credit card terms, when changes are made to a debt management plan and if your variable rate increases. What exactly is a debt management plan?

A debt management plan is an official agreement between a creditor and a debtor pertaining to a debt owed to the creditor by the debtor. The program is also designed to help the borrower pay off his or her outstanding debt faster. A debt management plan or debt relief plan is often a service a third-party company offers to someone who cannot afford to pay their debts on unsecured accounts. The third-party company (debt relief company) will collect the payment from the debtor and then distribute it to the creditor. A debtor often uses a debt relief company, because the company may help them to evaluate their debt, help the debtor to come up with a budget, establish a time frame to pay off their debt and negotiate with creditors on their behalf.

A debtor usually enters into a debt management plan with a creditor when they are facing some financial hardship that makes it difficult for them to make even the minimum payments on their loan or credit card. The debt management plan will most likely include an agreement to allow the debtor to make an affordable payment to the creditor. The creditor will probably agree to dramatically reduce the interest rate on the debtor balance or outright eliminate the interest on the debtor balance.

Chapter 8.

Effective Strategies for Repairing your Credit

Pay to Delete Strategy

If you have derogatory items in your credit report, you can opt to pay the unpaid credit balance only if the creditor agrees to delete the items from your credit report. As I already mentioned, don't agree for a $0 balance appearing on your credit report since this taints your reputation. This will ultimately improve your rating. Actually, the idea is to ensure that whatever amount you agree to pay doesn't show up as your last date of activity. If the creditor only cares about their money, why should they bother telling the world that you have finally paid?

In most instances, the creditors often write off debts within just 2 years of constant defaulting after which this information is sold in bulk to a collection company for some pennies of a dollar. This means that the collection companies will even be just fine if you even pay a fraction of what you ought to pay. Whatever you pay, they will still make money! This makes them open to negotiations such as pay to delete since they have nothing to lose anyway.

- Therefore, only use the pay to delete approach at this level and not any other. Actually, the only other way around it for the collection company is a judgment, which can be costly, so you have some advantage here.
- Additionally, use this strategy when new negative items start showing up in your report that could hurt your reputation as a credit consumer.
- Also, since the creditors will often sell the same information to multiple collection companies, you might probably start noting the same debt being reported by several companies; use pay to delete to get them off your report.
- You can also use this strategy if you have not been successful in getting items off your credit report using other methods. This is opting to go the dispute way might only make the process cyclic, which will be cumbersome, tiresome and frustrating; you don't want to get into this cycle.

Now that you know when to use this method, understanding how the entire process works is very critical. To start with, ensure that you get an acceptance in writing if they agree to your times; don't pay without the letter! After you agree, allow about 45 days for next credit report to be availed to you by your credit monitoring service. These companies have the legal power to initiate the deletion process so don't accept anything less such as updating the balance; it is either a deletion or nothing. If they try to stall the process by saying that they cannot delete, mention that it will only take about 5 minutes for them to fill the Universal Data Form. Don't worry if one company seems not to agree with your terms since another one will probably show up and will gladly take the offer.

In any case, what do they have to gain when they keep your debt when you are willing to pay? Remember that the records will just be in your records for 7 years so since 2 years are already past, these companies have no choice otherwise you can simply let the 7 years to pass! However, don't use this as an excuse for not paying your debts since the creditors can sue you to compel you to pay outstanding amounts. The aim of this process is to ensure that whatever bad experience you have with one creditor doesn't make the others to make unfavourable decisions on your part.

NOTE: don't be overly aggressive with creditors who have a lot to lose in the process especially the recent creditors since they can probably sue you. Your goal is only to be aggressive with creditors that are barred by the statute of limitation from suing you in court. You don't want to find yourself in legal trouble to add to your existing problems. Try and remain as smart as possible and make all the right moves to help you repair your credit at the earliest.

Pay to delete isn't the only option available to you; you can use other strategies to repair your credit.

Check for FDCPA (Fair Debt Collection Practices Act) Violations

The law is very clear on what collection agencies can do and what they cannot do as far as debt collection is concerned. For instance:

- They should not call you more than once in a day unless they can prove that it was accidentally dialled by their automated systems.
- They cannot call you before 8.00.am or after 9.00pm.
- They cannot threaten, belittle or yell at you to make you pay any outstanding debts.
- They cannot tell anyone else other than your spouse why they are contacting you.
- The best way to go about this is to let them know that you are recording all their calls.
- They cannot take more money from your account than you have authorized if they do an ACH.
- They are also not allowed to send you collection letters if you have already sent them a cease and desist order.

If you can prove that collection companies are in violation of the laws, you should file a complaint with the company then have your lawyer send proof indicating the violations; you can then request that any outstanding debt be forgiven. You need to understand that the law is on your side in such circumstances; actually, if the violations are major, the collection companies could be forced to pay fines of up to $10,000 for these violations.

So, if your debt is significantly lower than this, you could be on your way to having your debt cleared since these companies would rather pay your debt than pay the fine. Every violation of the Fair Debt Collection Practices Act is punishable by a fine of up to $1000, which is payable to you so don't just think of this as something that cannot amount to anything as far as repairing your credit is concerned.

Look for Errors on your Credit Reports

Your credit report should be free of errors. Even the slightest thing as reporting the wrong date of last activity on your credit report is enough to damage your credit. If the write off date is different from what has been reported, you can dispute the entry to have it corrected to reflect that actual status of your credit. However, keep in mind that the credit bureaus will in most instances confirm that the negative entry is correct even if this is not the case, which means that they will not remove the erroneous item.

You must put in efforts to get them on the right track. To get them to comply, you have to inform them that the law requires them to have preponderance of their systems in place to ensure that these errors do not arise. Therefore, the mere fact of confirming the initial error is not enough. Inform them about the Notice (Summons) and complaint to let them understand that you are serious about the matter. Once they have an idea of your stance, they will put in efforts to do the right thing. The thing is; the bureaus don't want any case to go to court since this could ultimately provide proof that their systems are weak or flawed, which means that they will probably be in some bigger problems.

So, try and drive a strong point across so that they understand you mean business. Mere exchange of emails will not do and you must send them details on how strong your case will be. This will make them understand their position and they will decide to help you to avoid going to court. This will, in turn, work to your advantage in making them to dig deeper into the issue. However, this method will only work if you are certain that an error was actually made. You will also require proof for it and cannot simply state that there was an error.

Request Proof of The Original Debt

If you are certain that the credit card has been written off for late payment, it is highly likely that the carriers (Capital One and Citibank) cannot find the original billing statements within 30 days, which they are required by the law to respond. This in effect allows you to have whatever entry you have disputed removed from the credit report as if it never happened.

Another handy approach is to request for the original contract that you signed to be provided to prove that you actually opened that particular credit card in the first instance. As you do this, don't just ask for "verification" since this just prompts the collection agency to "verify" that they actually received a request for collection on an account that has your name on it. Therefore, as a rule of thumb, ensure that you state clearly that you want them to provide proof of the debt including providing billing statements for the last several months and the original contract that you signed when opening the credit card account.

Pay the Original Creditor

When your debt is sold to collection agencies, you will probably risk having new items showing up on your credit report, which can further hurt your credit rating. However, you can stop that by sending a check with the full payment of any outstanding amount to the original creditor after which you just send a proof of payment to that collection agency and any other then request them to delete any derogatory items they have reported from your credit report.

It is always a good idea to be in direct contact with your creditor or creditors. In fact, many of these agencies will be fully equipped to cheat you and will follow through on plans to have your report show bad credit scores. It is up to you to try and remove these "middlemen" and do the payment yourself. You could also enter into an agreement to pay a portion of the money to the creditor as full payment for the sum (the pay to delete strategy).

Under the federal law, if the original creditor accepts any payment as full payment for any outstanding debt, the collection agency has to remove whatever they have reported. This will only work if the original creditor accepts the payment; it is possible for some of the checks you pay to the original creditor to be returned to you.

Chapter 9.

Controlling Various Kinds of Debt

Common Types of Debts

It depends on how you choose to see this. There are different kinds or types of debts. We will cut them into four groups to make this fun. Now, the first group.

1. Secured and Unsecured Loans.

Secured loans

> Secured loans are the types of debts you get by offering something as surety in case you don't pay that money up. As an example, if you are buying a house, a car, or getting a big work machine, you may opt for a loan when you don't have enough funds to clear the bills yourself. Often, that is a lot of money, and your credit company wants to be sure you're paying it all without complications. So, you are asked to mortgage some of your valued assets in turn. They keep the documents until your payment is complete. If you don't pay up, there are a few legal actions to make,

and they sell the assets. The norm is that you take this type of loan on significant assets.

Unsecured loans

Unsecured loans are the direct opposite of secured loans. You do not have to stake anything to access a loan like this. All you need is indicate your interest, submit your essential documents, and the loan is yours. The type of loan you're asking for is what determines what you will be submitting. For example, your credit report may just be enough to get you another credit card. You may have to drop a little deposit plus your credit report when you're signing up for some utilities. All of these have a little or minimal risk by the user. Only that you can cover simple services with this type of loan, no more. Now, you can imagine which weighs higher on a credit score ranked by FICO.

2. Fixed and Revolving Payment Method

Fixed Payment Method

A lot of times, your credit company lays out clear terms, duration, and method of payment to you. When this happens, we say you have got a fixed payment method. Usually, fixed payment methods attract fixed interests too. When you take part in a dealership deal, for example, you may be graced to get that money paid at a particular amount each month and a particular interest rate. Say, the car is worth a thousand USD. You are allowed to pay up in two years, with a total interest of 30%. That is pretty straightforward, right? That's just how fixed payment loans work. A mortgage is an example of fixed payment loans, so you might say they are pretty standard.

Revolving Payment Method:

These types of loans are those that swing like unpredictable bells. There are no exact modalities on most items. You simply take the loans and pay as you can. For example, you can pay when you have the funds; there is no exact deadline for payments. You don't get a limit to interest rates too. Often, your utility, as well as your credit card, fall into this category. This is the exact reason you draw up a credit card, and you can use the credit card as much as you like each month. You don't have to pay up that money when the month ends. You can pay a little now, a lot more over the coming months. But as FICO had earlier advised, it makes perfect sense to draw up only 30% or less of your credit limits. Expectedly, your interest rate is determined by how promptly you clear off that debt.

3. Good and Bad Loans

No questions, this list can't be closed if this group isn't here.

The Good Loans

Classifying loans as good or bad does not exist in official records. Maybe if it did, nobody would ever be excited to try out the bad ones. In any case, a good loan is any loan drawn to invest in resources that may become useful and available over a long period, sometimes, forever. Some of them are:

Mortgage: If it is damning to size up your mortgage and you are planning to hand over the building, my sincere suggestion is that you keep pulling through, and you remain upbeat. This is one of the loans you can't ever regret taking. It is glaring to anyone that houses are assets that you don't use up any moment soon. A house may get into a bad shape sometimes. That's normal. You are expected to keep it brimming with brightness naturally. If you do things right, you can't ever have to pay rents. You also have an asset you can risk getting huge loans to build your career. If things get worse, you can auction the house and restart your careers somewhere. However, you choose to see it, a loan drawn to get a house is a good one. Just be sure you can keep paying till the end before drawing the loan at all.

Student Loans: Well, you might hear someone say drawing student loan in insane. But if you look over the sayings, you'd have something different. You've got to get a good education, and you can't afford it at that moment. It makes perfect sense to tangle yourself in a loan, bag that degree, and pay back much more quickly. As you may fear, your first few years after school would be spent clearing your old debt. But you become free soon, and you'd have access to opportunities you may not have found without top training. From all viewpoints you see this, it is a win-win for all teams. So, I'd vote this as a good loan!

Business: Now, this is another perspective. If you are getting the loans to jack up your investments, you are settling for a good one too. It is undoubtedly a risk, since the business may pick up and may not. But if you probably play your cards right, your business can boom, and that is the start of a goal you didn't see coming.

So, Bad Loans?

Auto loans: For a fact, you must be curious to know why auto loans should be tagged a bad debt, isn't it? I bet! Well, it is. Auto Loans, dealerships, and whatever kind of car loan you get into is a bad loan. This is because cars are not assets that can be used for a long while. If you sign a two or five-year loan deal, your car is already developing some sorts of problems. So, you'd have to spend on it, and at that same time, pay your auto loans. It would be a mess in a few years.

Credit Card Loans: Credit Card Loans are probably the worst you can take. They can't be used to get important stuff. And either you take note or not, your debt is on the rise with every month you forgot to clear up.

Most Other loans: Most of the other types of loans fall into this category, especially those you draw from friends and family. They are often not precisely significant and should be avoided. Except, of course, they are critical to you, and you are sure there's some way you can quickly pay it all back.

How to Control Your Credit

Regardless of what credit types you have drawn, it is vital to monitor and control it all before it gets out of hand. Even if it's slipped a bit, the best option you've got is to find some way to monitor and control it. Hence, I'll be showing you some easy and practical ways in the next few lines. Here;

1. Don't let things slip off: That's the first rule. Prevention is way better than cure. It stands to reason that if you can plan appropriately and watch out for sinking moments, you shouldn't have to fight to save your credit score fiercely. All you need is to do the math. Where are you heading to? What are your chances of hitting it big or terribly crashing? What would you have to do to avoid falling into a debt pit and struggling to pay up? Several things we might say. Your first job is to find those targets and set them working.

2. Don't spend payments: Pending payments only increase your penalties. Whether for fixed and revolving debts. So, with the facts that you should avoid pending your payments. Clear them off the instant you are able to.

3. Don't toy with revolving debts: Revolving debts are full of surprises. You would usually assume they are the littlest, and so, they can be paid after the much bigger debts. In reality, your revolving debts (like your credit cards) cart away more than your fixed debts. They tend to increase all the time, and there's a high potential for interest increase too, which doesn't happen in fixed credit cases. Hence, it washes that you should pay them up before considering some other debts at all. Don't delay others too!

If you do the math and your revolving debts are out, you will have a concrete idea of how to tackle the only other debts you have left. This itself is an acute style of controlling debts that you didn't notice. Now you know, cheers.

Let's Get Learning Effective Strategies.

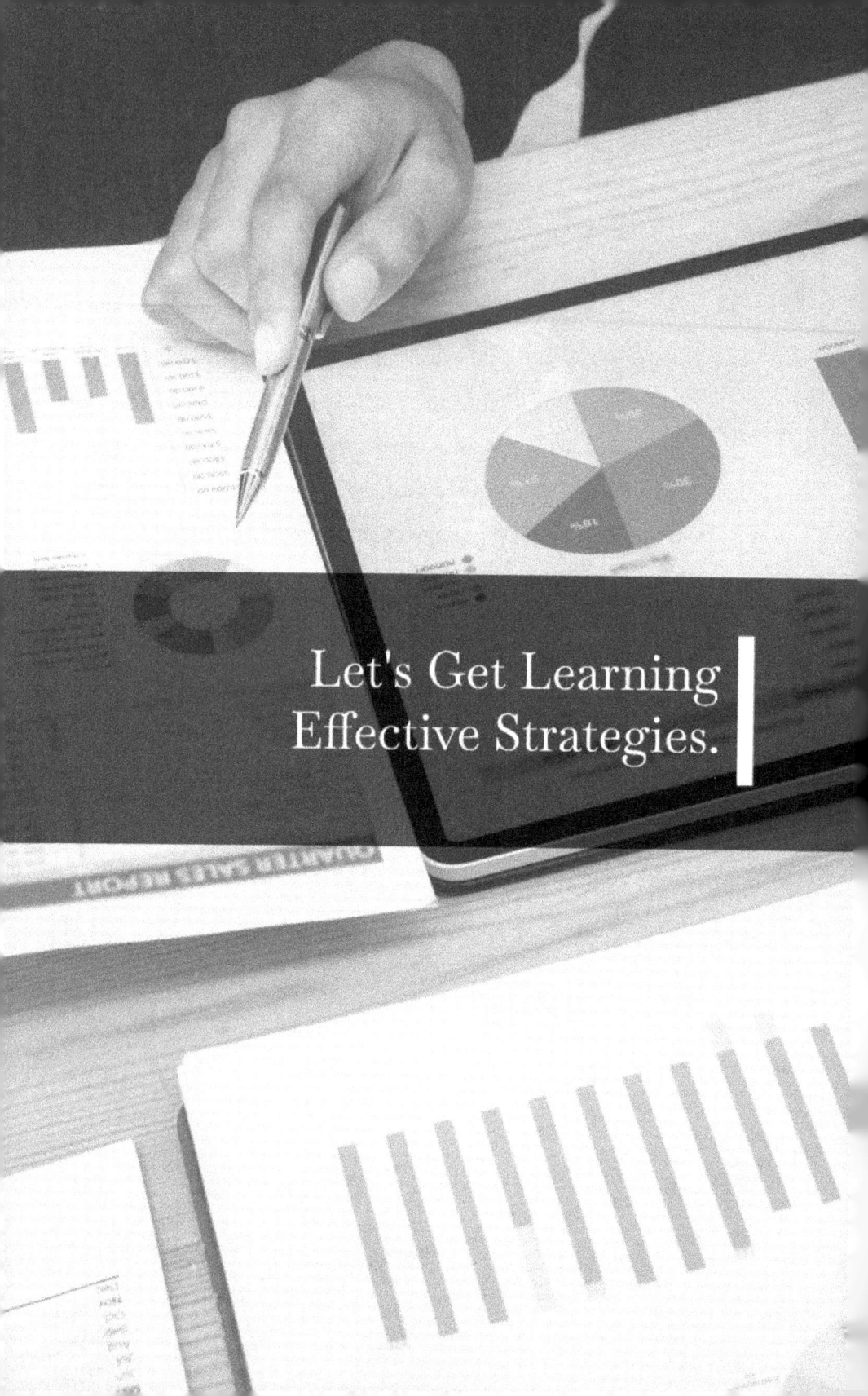

Chapter 10.

Guaranteed Methods to Protect Credit Score

Do Not Fully Use Your Credit Cards

30% of your score is how you use your credit. For example, having a credit card with a $10,000 limit is amazing! You can do whatever you want with it, and trust me, that is something I often did. But, that is actually another item that can gravely affect your credit score. You want to make sure you are only using up to 30% of your credit card. "But Alan, what is the point of having a $10,000 card limit if I can only use $3,000?!" Great question! Let me explain it in more detail. By the end of the billing month, you only want to have, at most, 30% on your credit card balance. You can use the full amount of the credit card if you want, just pay it off before the end of the billing month.

A simple and fun example goes like this, I want to be a baller and buy 500 large pizzas for a block party, at the cost of $15 each (and I was in some weird loophole where taxes were exempt, I would have placed $7,500 on my credit card, even though I already had $2000 on my card. That is clearly 95% of my card limit! But, if I turned around and paid everything off my credit card, the end of my billing month would show that I had $2,000 debt. My credit score will not be negatively affected by buying food for the best block party in existence! Now, in a perfect world, paying off your cards in its entirety by the end of the billing month is by far the best thing you can do. Pay what you can but stay under 30%!

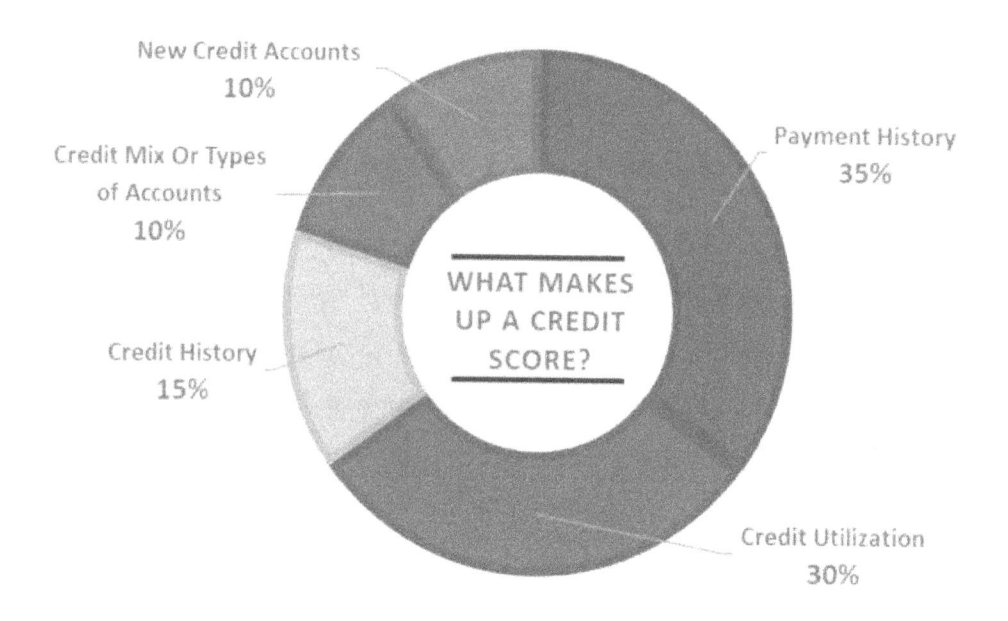

WHAT MAKES UP A CREDIT SCORE?

- New Credit Accounts 10%
- Credit Mix Or Types of Accounts 10%
- Credit History 15%
- Payment History 35%
- Credit Utilization 30%

Hacking Your Way to That Perfect Score

The below image is a fantastic simple guide to climbing up that credit score ladder. Now, that looks nice, but what exactly is considered "excellent" credit? Well, after searching and searching, it seems as though you are considered Excellent, when your credit score reaches 760. That number seems to be the number that is in the goldilocks zone in the credit score world. With an Excellent credit score rating, you will have the best interest rates, you will have the least amount of issues attempting to get loans, and you most definitely will never have to leave a deposit whenever you want to turn on your utilities at the brand new home you will buy with that amazing mortgage rate you will get!

	Excellent	Good	Fair	Poor	Very Poor
Credit Card Utilization (High)	0-9%	10-29%	30-49%	50-74%	75%+
Payment History (High)	100%	99%	98%	97%	<97%
Derogatory Marks (High)	0	-	1	2-3	4+
Age of Credit History (Medium)	9+ years	7-8 years	5-6 years	2-4 years	< 2 years
Total Accounts (Low Impact)	21+	11-20	-	6-10	0-5
Credit Inquiries (Low Impact)	0	1-2	3-4	5-8	9+

We need to make sure we cover everything. If you have missed/late payment marks on your credit report, reach out to that credit card company and ask them to get them removed! Let them know of the reason why you were not able to pay them on time and then let them know of the good standing you are with them while letting them know of your goals of improving your credit score. I have gotten 3 late payment marks taken off within a month!

If you had collection marks on your credit report, and you went through the process of trying to remove them and you still ended up paying, wait a few months and send them a letter asking to get it removed. This may work. But if you really want it to work, send a lot of letters, 2-3 a week until someone who gets paid $10 an hour does not want to deal with it anymore and removes the mark from the credit report. I have done it once, and though at first, I felt shameful, 3 months later I no longer had it! I must have broken through to someone! Win!

If you are new to getting credit, having 9-year worth of credit history will definitely be a difficult task, you may have to wait. But in that time, follow this guide and make sure you are making all your payments on time! For those of you who have been around for quite some time, do not close your credit cards. If you have to, then please be wary, but I would hold onto any and all credit cards and never close them. If you do not want to use them anymore, just don't use them.

Chapter 11.

The Credit Bureau

Credit bureaus are privately held, billion-dollar organizations whose primary reason for existing is to make cash; that is what revenue driven organizations do right? They keep data that lenders furnish them - regardless of whether accurate or inaccurate - about our credit association with them and sell it. Basic, right? This straightforward plan of action generates over $4 Billion per year!

One wellspring of income for them originates from selling the information on our credit reports to different lenders, managers, insurance agencies, credit card organizations - and whoever else you approve to see your credit information. In addition to the fact that they provide them with crude data; yet they likewise sell them various methods for examining the data to decide the risk of stretching out credit to us. In addition to trading our information to lenders, they likewise sell our information to us - credit scores, credit observing administrations, extortion security, wholesale fraud prevention - interestingly enough this region has quickly gotten perhaps the greatest wellspring of income. Furthermore, those pre-endorsed offers in our letter drop each week, or garbage mail? That's right; they got our information from the credit bureaus as well. Organizations buy in to an assistance provided by the three credit bureaus that sell them a rundown of consumer's credit information that fit a pre-decided criterion.

Presently, as opposed to prevalent thinking, credit bureaus don't have any contribution on whether you ought to be endorsed for a loan or not; that is absolutely based on the credit criteria of the lender you're working with. However, by utilizing the entirety of the information that has been set on your credit report (personal information, payment history, and credit propensities) and FICO's technique for scoring that data, they do tell them with how creditworthy you are.

What Credit Bureaus Do?

Credit bureaus collect information from various sources in accordance with consumer information. The activity is done for various reasons and includes data from singular consumers. Included is the information concerning a people charge payments and their getting. Utilized for evaluating creditworthiness, the information provides lenders with an outline of your accounts if a loan repayment is required. The interest rates charged on a loan are additionally worked out concerning the kind of credit score shown by your experience. It is thusly not a uniform procedure, and your credit report is the significant instrument that affects future loans.

Based on risk-based valuing, it pegs various risks on the various customers in this manner deciding the cost you will acquire as a borrower. Done as credit rating, it is an assistance provided to various interested parties in the public. Terrible credit histories are affected for the most part by settled court commitments which mark you for high interest rates every year. Duty liens and bankruptcies, for example, shut you out of the conventional credit lines and may require a great deal of arrangement for any loan to be offered by the bank.

Bureaus collect and examine credit information including financial data, personal information, and elective data. This is given by various sources generally marked data furnishers. These have an exceptional association with the credit bureaus. An average gathering of data furnishers would comprise of creditors, lenders, utilities, and debt collection agencies. Pretty much any association which has had payment involvement in the consumer is qualified including courts. Any data collected for this situation is provided to the credit bureaus for grouping. When it is accumulated, the data is placed into specific repositories and files claimed by the bureau. The information is made accessible to customers upon request. The idea of such information is important to lenders and managers.

The information is in this manner material in various conditions; credit evaluation andbusiness thought are simply part of these. The consumer may likewise require the information to check their individual score and the home proprietor may need to check their inhabitants report before renting an apartment. Since the market is saturated by borrowers, the scores will, in general, be robotic. Straightforward examination would deal with this by giving the client a calculation for speedy appraisal. Checking your score once every other year should deal with errors in your report.

Individuals from the public are qualified for one free credit report from every one of the significant bureaus. This is organized in the Fair Credit Report Act, FCTA. Other government rules associated with the assurance of the consumer incorporate Fair and Accurate Credit Transaction Act, Fair Credit Billing Act and Regulation B. Statutory bodies have additionally been made for the regulation of the credit bureaus. The Fair-Trade Commission serves to as a controller for the consumer credit report agencies while the Office of the Comptroller of Currency fills in as a manager of all banks going about as furnishers.

Choose A Debt Payoff Method That Works For You

Chapter 12.

How to Overcome Credit Card Debt

What is a Credit Card Debt?

When you incur a credit card debt, you actually keep borrowing money every month, and that is why it is also known as revolving debt. But it is only good until you have the capacity to repay them but when you can't, the debt keeps accumulating. When compared to the loan accounts, you can actually keep using your credit card accounts for an indefinite period of time. On the other hand, in the case of instalment loan accounts, after you have cleared out the entire balance, the account will be closed.

Another thing that you should keep in mind about a credit card debt is that it is an unsecured type of debt. In simpler terms, there is nothing that the company can seize, like a house or a card, even when you have failed to repay them. But yes, if you are not able to repay the money you borrowed from the credit card, it is going to affect your credit score drastically.

How Is Credit Card Debt Accumulated?

When you get a credit card, you will see that there will be a due date within which you have to clear the entire balance that you have accumulated on your credit card, and if you fail to do so, you will be accumulating debt. There is a term called APR or Annual Percentage Rate and this is a rate of interest that is charged on your debt when it keeps accumulating one month after the other. The APR that you will be charged may not be the same with someone else's and this is because it keeps differing with your credit history, the bank issuer, and the type of card that you have.

The benchmark fed funds rate of the Federal Reserve and the prime rate of the credit card interests is somewhat tied, and that is the average value. The credit card debt will increase or decrease with respect to any changes in the target rate made by the Fed.

Now, I want to give you an even clearer picture of how this debt accumulates. For starters, there is a minimum payment that you will have to pay every month whenever you use your credit card to make purchases. This payment is calculated based on a certain percentage (with some additional interest charges) of your balance. If you pay this amount in full, then well and good, but if you don't, then you will be liable to interest. So, the interest will increase if you pay even lesser. The reason behind this is that the nature of credit card interests is compounding so the interest keeps accruing. Thus, if you take a longer time to clear off the debts, then you will owe a huge amount of money to the company, which is much more than what you owed before.

What Happens After 7 Years?

This is basically a time limit until which a record is shown in a credit report. But there are certain other negative issues that will stay in your credit report even after seven years, for example, certain judgments, tax liens that are unpaid, and bankruptcy.

But you also have to keep in mind that if any debt is unpaid, then it is not exactly going to vanish even after seven years. Even if the credit report does not list it, you will still owe that money to the lender.

There are several other legal ways that can be implemented by the lenders, creditors, and debt collectors to collect the debt that you haven't paid. Some of these methods include a court giving permission to garnish your wages, sending letters, calling you, and so on. In some cases, you can even be sued.

One thing that you benefit because of this seven- years rule is that when the debt is no longer visible on your credit report, it cannot affect your credit score. Thus, you can actually have a better chance of gaining back a good score. Another thing to keep in mind is that this seven-years term is only for the negative information on your report and not the position information because they will stay on the report forever. You should keep an eye out after the seven- year mark as to whether the credit bureaus have removed that information or not. They usually do it automatically, but in case they don't then you will have to raise a dispute.

Many people have this question of what happens to their debt if they accidentally die. Well, in that case, it will be your estate that will be used to pay the debt off. Remember that the debt will not be shoved in someone else's hand in your family because whatever money you owe, it is your debt and not anyone else's. And so, whatever you had, like your accounts and assets will then be used for clearing the debt. And after that, if anything remains from your assets, your heir will receive it.

How to Eliminate Credit Card Debt?

Now that you have a basic idea of what a credit card debt is, let us talk about how you can eliminate it.

Start Eliminating High-Interest Debts First

When you are trying to eliminate your credit card debt, the biggest obstacle that will stand in your way are the ones that carry a very high rate of interest. Sometimes, the rate of interest can even be in double- digits, sometimes as high as 22%. In that case, paying it off can be a really difficult task. But the reason why I am asking you to start eliminating them first because when you will have cleared these debts, you will have a greater amount of money left in your hand at the end of each month.

Another thing that you could do, but only if you have enough credit available, is to apply for a new credit card. But this should be a zero-interest one. Once you get it, transfer the balance to eliminate the high- interest debt. Yes, I know that some of you might be thinking that it is not a sensible thing to do to apply for another credit card and that is why I will be asking you to get it only if you think you have enough self- restraint not to buy a bunch of stuff that you don't need.

Keep Making Small Payments

Quite contrary to the technique I mentioned above is another technique which is called the snowflake technique. With this process, you will be making small payments towards your debt every time you get some extra cash in hand. Whatever payment you are making, it does not matter as long as you keep paying.

You can pay $10, or you can pay $20 but at the end of the year, you will find that you have reduced about $1000 simply by paying such small amounts almost every day, even if you are paying $2 on any day.

People often ignore this method, thinking that it will be only small amounts but you should not make the mistake of overlooking these small amounts as they have quite the power in them. When you are making these small payments, it would feel as if they are not even leaving any dent but with time, they will sum up and cause a considerable effect on your debt.

Preventive Measures to Avoid Credit Card Debt

Have an Emergency Fund

Think about a situation when you have encountered a problem that requires you to spend a lot of money, for example, a car repair or job loss or medical emergencies. In such a situation, what you need is an emergency fund, but when people don't have that, they resort to credit cards for help.

But why arrive at such a situation when you can build an emergency fund that will cover at least six months' expenses. If you are finding it difficult to come up with a huge amount, then start by accumulating $500 and then work your way up to $1000. A fund of this size will help you to figure out any small expenses that crop up overnight. Take your time to build your emergency fund so that you do not have to rely on debt ever.

But Only Those Things That You Can Afford

When you have a credit card in hand, it can get really tempting, and you start buying whatever you think you want. But take a step back and think whether you can really afford that item if you did not have a credit card. If not, then don't buy it now. Make a goal to save the money required for purchasing that item instead of buying it on credit.

Don't Transfer Balance If Not Necessary

Some people have this habit of clearing their balance with a higher credit card but such repeated balance transferring can actually backfire at you. When you keep transferring balanced without keeping track of your activities, you might end up with an ever- increasing balance and you will also have to clear the fee requires for all those transfers.

Try Not Taking Out a Cash Advance

Sometimes, you may be in the moment, and you were not thinking clearly so, you decide to take a cash advance. But you have to remember and remind yourself that a cash advance comes with very hefty transaction fees and you are not even going to get a grace period in which you can avoid the charges. Moreover, you will have to realize that you are getting into credit card debt if you have started making cash advanced. The moment you see it happening, you will have to start working on that emergency fund and also tweak your budget.

Lastly, I would like to say that no matter how many measures you take, try avoiding increasing your credit cards unnecessarily because the more the number of credit cards, the more you will have to stop yourself from overspending.

Chapter 13.

Credit Repair from Scratch

How to Build a Credit Score from scratch?

There are several ways and all of them are effective.

1. The first is to open a bank account. Having an account open will not increase your score, but it will give you a starting point to show regular income. After a few months, you can ask your bank (remember to show off your best smile) what services they offer to increase your Credit Score. My bank, for example, offers a mini-loan of $ 500 tied up to be returned in 6 months. It means that you deposit $ 500, they re-loan them to you at a favorable rate and when, in 6 months, you finish paying the instalments, they give you back the $ 500 in the barrel. Practically in 6 months, you paid interest as a "tax" with the sole purpose of accumulating points. To put it in simpler words: from 500 and 500 you return, then you pay 500 in instalments + interest and you return 500 at the end. It is an expense, but this type of loan guarantees you a considerable accumulation of points, but only if you are regular in payments.

2.   The second, and in my opinion the best, is to apply for a Secured Credit Card. Unlike traditional credit cards, you do not have to show any kind of entry to get approval, but you also have a usage limit. The only thing required is a deposit which is returned to you after a year of regular use. Until a couple of years ago, the deposit was around 200 euros, but with the debt problems that developed after the recession, all the major credit companies have lowered the costs. For example, I applied with Capital One (but there are many others like Discover). The deposit was only $ 49 and the card limit was $ 200 a month with the option of 2% cash back on gas or restaurant expenses. I started using it regularly every month ONLY for these two things and, after a year, my Credit Score was already considered very good, they also returned the deposit and the cash back and the credit limit rose to 500 dollars after only six months. We clarify that you are not obliged to use it only for these things, but I have limited myself for two reasons. The first is to accumulate cash back (i.e. a refund) at the end of the year. The second is to make sure I never use more than 30% of the card limit. Which brings me to the next point.

3.   Never exceed 30% of the credit card limit. Believe it or not, it is essential that you show that you do not need a credit card to pay for your things, but that you use it only when strictly necessary or as an accurate choice. The more you use it constantly the better, but judiciously.

4.   Pay your instalments regularly. All the above points have absolutely no value if you are not constant in payments. No one here scales your loan or credit card debts from your salary. It is your responsibility to remember when you have to pay or set up an automatic payment from your bank account. I decided to set up automatic payments. As long as he has a good memory, you never know what can happen that can put you off your mind on the expiry day. So, I strongly suggest you do the same because even a missed payment will negatively affect your score.

5.   Vary the types of debt as much as you can. If you can make the Secured Card And the mini-loan with the bank at the same time, do it. The more options you have, the faster your Credit Score will grow. Of course, always keep in mind that if you don't pay on time, they show up at home with the Pit bulls (so to speak or almost). So, if you're not sure you can do better, don't risk it and wait a little longer.

6.   Add your name to someone else's credit card as an "authorized user". If, for example, if you are married to an American who has had much more time than you to accumulate a decent score (as in my case), it might be a good idea for him to indicate you as an authorized user of his credit cards. This does not mean that you will actually have to use his credit cards, but the more his score improves, the more he will positively influence yours. Be careful though! If you go down, he comes down with you. This type of choice involves a fat, large demonstration of trust so be careful not to betray

it. If you mess up the Credit Score that has been sweating so much since he was in swaddling clothes, well I wouldn't want to be in your shoes!

7.   Check your Credit Score regularly to make sure there are no problems you are unaware of and have such nasty surprises. Even a late paid bill can affect your payer profile. Now pay attention to the following because it's important. There are several ways to check where you are with the economic 'pregnancy'. The first is to apply here for your Annual Credit Report, but you are entitled to a free check only once a year. The second is to check directly in Credit Bureaus such as Trans union, Equifax or Experian. Also in these cases, you can have a free check per year, or pay a monthly instalment to keep your score constantly under control. Obviously, the annual checks have their advantages, but be careful not to take too much advantage of their services. Believe it or not, every time you request a check this will lower your Credit Score. Crazy, right? And this brings me to the only sensible solution that remains to keep the score under control.

8.   Download the free Credit Karma app. Not only does it constantly give you a detailed report of your score, but also what has positively or negatively influenced, which credit cards or loans are best suited to your situation, your progress, and many other functions. It's all free and, although not updated to the minute, rather accurate. It does not lower your Credit Score and also offers you many other services such as online and free tax returns. Due to Credit Karma, other major credit companies have also had

to adjust to offer the Credit Score free check. For example, Capital One and Discover have now integrated this service into their offers (although in a more limited way being a cost to them).

If you follow these tips in a year you can afford to ask for a car loan without having to pay disproportionate interest or even more, depending on your income and your general receivables/payables situation. This reminds me of how important it is to start as soon as possible. Remember that this is the first thing they look at when you need to apply for a loan!

Conclusion

One of the tools you can use to your advantage is the free investment or personal loan; however, it has certain restrictions. Never buy a car with this type of credit, since there is a specific credit for it. A car loan has more convenient interest rates and benefits than a personal loan. It is also not good for paying off another credit, except for the famous "debt purchase". Don't enter the so-called "carousel", in other words, do not take out one loan to pay off another, unless it is a debt consolidation: take out a loan to pay off several debts and keep just one. It is also not recommended to complete the down payment on a home loan; always save for that type of purchase.

You shouldn't lend to other people; even though you know them, they're not you and they can probably fail to pay on time. Easier to repay that loan? Get lower rates by opening an account in the chosen entity, especially if it is an account where your credits are saved; you would have access to lower interest rates. It helps to have a credit card from that entity. A good way to reduce interest on your loan is to pay extraordinary fees, that is, pay double fees in some month and generate savings. Remember: having pre-approved loans and cards is a good indicator in your credit history; for different entities, you are a low risk person and you have a solvent economic situation.

If you are denied of getting a credit, is maybe because it exceeds your possibility to pay or maybe you cannot prove that you have enough incomes to pay for it. Ask for the reason of the denial. In this way, you will be able to see the improvements you can make, such as reducing your debts and pending loans to settle, increasing your income for a greater possibility to pay, or revisiting your credit report to request again the amount to be borrowed.

These habits will allow you to improve financially, while your credit history benefits.

You must save money. If you want to see your money grow, you have to make sacrifices. Find all the ways to make a living. Let me give you an example. I have a coach, who warned me that two health conditions are the most expensive: coronary heart disease and mental health-related illnesses. Even if you have a humble job, you will have to save for one or both conditions. I won't tell you which one I have, but I can assure you that the cost of medicines and private medical consultation is high.

Quit the job you have. Currently, a stable job in some countries is not secure. There are many graduated people in my profession and every day there are more staff cuts in the workplaces. Entrepreneurship is the key. As an example, from my parents, my mother is obstetrician and my dad is an electronic technician and chauffeur. One day they stopped being employees of the government and started several entrepreneurships: private transportation, a convenience store, food concessionaire, lender, home installations. These ventures have brought them more income than their careers. Today, they continue to invest in real estate while receiving residual income from rentals of apartments and shops.

One of my grandparents worked in a textile factory for 40 years as a machine technician. Even though he bought two houses he worked for 40 years. He worked even on holidays, didn't saw his family as much as he wanted to and had to rest after so many years of work. I particularly, bid farewell to an expensive lifestyle: I bid farewell to that pitcher with the head of a cat and to that luxurious first-class journeys. Finally: Bill Gates, Steve Jobs, Michael Dell, left their comfortable life and set out on their own path. And you, what do you need to start creating your financial freedom? It's up to you.

Dave R. W. Graham

The Best Dispute Letter Templates for You.

BONUS:
The Best Templates You Can Use to Work with Section 609

Dispute Letter Templates

Letter 1: Affidavit of unknown inquiries

EQUIFAX
P.O. box 740256
ATLANTA GA 30374

My name Is John William; my current address is 6767. W Phillips Road, San Jose, CA 78536, SSN: 454-02-9928, Phone: 415-982-3426, Birthdate: 6-5-1981

I checked my credit reports and noticed some inquiries from companies that I did not give consent to access my credit reports, I am very concerned about all activity going on with my credit reports these days. I immediately demand the removal of these inquiries to avoid any confusion as I DID NOT initiate these inquires or give any form of consent electronically, in person, or over the phone. I am fully aware that without permissible purpose no entity is allowed to pull my credit unless otherwise noted in section 604 of the FCRA.

DAVE ROBERT WARREN GRAHAM

The following companies did not have permission to request my credit report:

CUDL/FIRST CALIFORNIA ON 6-15-2017

CUDL/NASA FEDERAL CREDIT UNION ON 6-15-2017

LOANME INC 3-14-2016

CBNA on 12-22-2017

I once again demand the removal of these unauthorized inquiries immediately.

(Signature)

THANK YOU

Letter 2: Affidavit of suspicious addresses

1-30-2018

ASHLEY WHITE

2221 N ORANGE AVE APT 199

FRESNO CA 93727

PHONE: 559-312-0997

SSN: 555-59-4444

BIRTHDATE: 4-20-1979

EQUIFAX

P.O. box 740256

ATLANTA GA 30374

To whom it may concern:

I recently checked a copy of my credit report and noticed some addresses reporting that do not belong to me or have been obsolete for an extended period of time. For the safety of my information, I hereby request that the following obsolete addresses be deleted from my credit reports immediately;

4488 N white Ave apt 840 Fresno, CA 93722

4444 W Brown Ave apt 1027 Fresno CA 93722

13330 E Blue Ave Apt 189 Fresno CA 93706

I have provided my identification card and social security card to verify my identity and current address. Please notify any creditors who may be reporting any unauthorized past accounts that are in connection with these mentioned addresses as I have exhausted all of my options with the furnishers.

(Your signature)

This letter is to get a response from the courts to show the credit bureaus that you have evidence that they cannot legally validate the Bankruptcy

Letter 3: Affidavit of James Robert

U.S BANKRUPTCY COURT
700 STEWART STREET 6301
SEATTLE, WA 98101
RE: BANKRUPTCY (164444423TWD SEATTLE, WA)

To whom it may concern:

My Name is JAMES ROBERT my mailing address is 9631 s 2099h CT Kent, WA 99999.

I recently reviewed my credit reports and came upon the above referenced public record. The credit agencies have been contacted and they report in their investigation that you furnished or reported to them that the above matter belongs to me. This act may have violated federal and Washington state privacy laws by submitting such information directly to the credit agencies, Experian, Equifax, and Trans Union via mail, phone or fax.

I wish to know if your office violated Washington State and federal privacy laws by providing information on the above referenced matter via phone, fax or mail to Equifax, Experian or Trans Union.

Please respond as I have included a self-addressed envelope,

Thank You (your signature)

Letter 4: Affidavit for account validation

First letter you send to the credit bureaus for disputes

1-18-2019

TRANSUNION

P.O. BOX 2000

CHESTER PA 19016

To Whom It May Concern:

My name is John Doe, SSN:234-76-8989, my current address is 4534. N Folk street Victorville, CA 67378, Phone: 310-672-0929 and I was born on 4-22-1988.

After checking my credit report, I have found a few accounts listed above that I do not recognize. I understand that before any account or information can be furnished to the credit bureaus; all information and all accounts must be 100% accurate, verifiable and properly validated. I am not disputing the existence of this debt, but I am denying that I am the responsible debtor. I am also aware that mistakes happen, I believe these accounts can belong to someone else with a similar name or with my information used without my consent either from the furnisher itself or an individual.

I am demanding physical documents with my signature or any legally binding instruments that can prove my connection to these erroneous entries, Failure to fully verify that these accounts are accurate is a violation of the FCRA and must be removed or it will continue to damage my ability to obtain additional credit from this point forward.

I hereby demand that the accounts listed above be legally validated or be removed from my credit report immediately.

Thank You (Your signature)

Letter 5: Sample Dispute Letter to Credit Bureaus

Date

(Sent certified mail with a return receipt requested)

Your Name

Your Address

Your City, State, Zip Code

( ) Insert name of bureau: Equifax, Experian, or Trans Union
Address
City, State, Zip Code

To Whom It May Concern:

This letter is to request that you investigate inaccurate information contained in my ( ) credit file. (Fill in the blank with Equifax, Experian, or Trans Union, depending on the credit bureau to which you are writing.) The information I am disputing pertains to the ( ) of the account listed below: (Fill in the blank with the word "ownership" or "status," depending on the type of dispute.)

( ) Account, with the account number ending as ( ) (Put the account name and the last four digits of the account in the respective blanks.)

The data reported about me is erroneous because (). (Insert your own reason or fill in the blank, as appropriate, with one of the following reasons: "This is not my account"; "I have never paid late"; "I paid this account in full"; "This account was included in my bankruptcy"; "The balance shown is incorrect"; or "This account was opened fraudulently, and I am the victim of identity theft.")

Indicated below are my full name, date of birth, Social Security number, and address for the past two years:

Full Name:
Date of Birth:
Social Security Number:
Address, City, State, Zip Code:

Also enclosed is a copy of () (Insert "my driver's license," "a recent utility bill," or "a recent credit-card statement.") so that you can verify my address and identity. Please investigate this matter promptly and delete the incorrect information as required by law.

Sincerely,

Your Signature
Your Name

Enclosures (List what you are enclosing. Only send copies, not originals. Also mention whether you are providing any supporting documents to prove your claim. By law this information must be forwarded by the credit bureau to the creditor, bill collector, or furnisher of the erroneous information.)

BOOK 3:
THE BEST CREDIT HABITS
(*UNPUBLISHED WORK*)

Find Out in Simple Steps How To Manage Your Credit and Get A Happier Financial Life.

Introduction

A credit score is simply an endeavor to rank your creditworthiness with a goal number. It used to be that in the event that you needed a credit you would go into the bank, and in the event that you had a decent remaining in the network, or if the advance official had a positive sentiment about you, you could get an advance. Clearly, there is a blemish in that framework; anyone, regardless of how very much regarded, can be an awful credit hazard. Along these lines, by computing the impact of various factors on your capacity to reimburse, the credit offices concocted a way that tries to treat everyone decently.

There are a few distinct things considered by the credit offices when making sense of a score. Fortunately, a large portion of them is good judgment. The one thing that makes up the majority of your score is your installment history. Along these lines, probably the best thing you can begin doing (or keep doing) is taken care of the entirety of your tabs on schedule. Next, don't owe excessively. Your obligation to-salary proportion ought to be at 25% or less. That implies the sum you owe ought not to surpass 25% of your pay. Try not to open such a large number of records in a brief timeframe, and don't lose an excessive amount of either. Possibly apply for an advance or credit in the event that you genuinely need it. As referenced, a large portion of these things are sound judgment, and they will consistently go far towards improving your general budgetary wellbeing.

Is a credit score actually that significant, all things considered, it's just a number, isn't that so? Right, however, it's an inescapable number at that. The most notable model is the banks. They will utilize your credit score to decide if you get an advance, and assuming this is the case, what terms you will get. Be that as it may, your credit score is utilized by much something other than moneylenders. On the off chance that you go after a position, your potential business may pull your credit report before settling on their employing choice. Proprietors use credit scores to see who they will lease to. Insurance agencies use them as a component of their hazard evaluation before offering you an arrangement.

There is no uncertainty that your credit score is significant. Since you have more data on what it's everything about, you can find a way to maintain or improve your score.

Truth be told, learning about credit and finance can be an intimidating task, I believe one should seek to understand anything they choose to participate in, and to be honest, we don't have a choice when it comes to credit. Why not have the knowledge and understanding of credit regardless of any trade or career you are in or will pursue credit can always be used as a tool of leverage no matter how much money you have or make. Pay attention to how even the wealthy people secure mortgages to purchase their property and pay interest while still building equity.

Chapter 1.

How to Get Started To Build Your Credit

Credit card debts are probably seen as something that cause great distress. The good news is that you can break free from the bondage of debt. Apart from rebuilding your credit history, your mentality should be focused on getting out of debt and building wealth. Dumping debt is empowering. And you have the power to stay out of debt if you really want to.

The following are added information on how you can rebuild your credit and finally proclaim yourself, debt free.

Use Good Credit to Leverage Your Way Up

If you have gone through a bad experience about credit cards, you would probably associate the word "credit" with the word "bad". Good credit breeds good credit. Part of the technique is to use your credit and be wise enough to become a person of good standing. With a good credit rating, you are able to get the best interest rates on your loans and credit cards. Having good credit standing helps you become more aware of your status and keep to it. Collection calls are now a thing of the past. The constant feeling of worrying how to settle your monthly dues are no longer a major concern. Bills are paid off and you feel a certain kind of control, freedom, and peace of mind.

There Needs to Be an Activity and Constant Update

In order to rebuild your credit, do not let old information sit for a long time. Your credit report should always have recent activities listed for at least six months. Be active and generate good information. There has to be timely and consistent pattern of payments so you can be flagged for consistent payments. Having regular activity means your credit report gets fresh update on a monthly basis.

Get a Secured Credit Card

This is another way to prove that you are credit worthy. If getting a regular credit card is not possible, you may get a secured card. It works in a way that you deposit a certain amount in the bank, and in essence, allow you to borrow it back. Your credit limit depends on the money that you have deposited. Pay your monthly fees on time and request for a regular card after a year of no delay payments. Finally, the more important part is that you confirm with the credit union if they turn in your good standing information to the credit reporting agencies. Remember your purpose in getting the card – build your credit rating. So if they are not going to turn up on the credit report, this whole thing of rebuilding your credit is pointless.

Borrow a Small Installment Loan from Your Trusted Bank

This is another way towards a stellar credit report. It may seem odd at first but know that credit scores are calculated based on having different kinds of loans and not just credit cards. You can just opt to borrow a small amount from the bank and keep the length of the loan for at least a year. The goal is to establish a new credit path and have regular activity to spark your credit score.

Co-Sign a Loan with Someone

Just a word of caution: co-sign a loan with someone whom you know is responsible enough to take on debt and pay for it. Remember, when you co-sign, you share the debt. And, if they fail to repay the debt, the lending bank will come to you for full payment. Also, if your spouse or a family member is an authorized user of your credit card, you can make him/her a joint account holder. Getting credit under each person's name can give you good credit.

Completely Eliminate Your Debt for Life

If there is one method that would cure your debts and worries away that would have to be debt elimination. You can do this by allotting money meant for your bills. Or, if you have saved up for the rainy days, now is the time to take that out and lessen your debts. Paying them could save you with hundreds and thousands of dollars on interest rates. You would not want to pay high interest rates for life, don't you?

Apply the Debt Reduction Method

All you have to do is prepare a simple draft of your income statement showing your net worth, a balance sheet, and two letters from your CPA. Showing concrete statements is one of your most powerful tools in reducing your debt drastically. Just do not forget to consult your financial adviser about this.

Always Check for Identity Theft

There is a high probability that there could be an unexplained item (s) in your credit report that does not belong to you. Sad fact is that it is a bad credit score. If this happens, you could be denied credit and you are going to pay for it. So if there is something mysterious that you see in your credit report, call the credit card company immediately. You need to act fast because you could be a victim of identity theft. It is a real threat.

Avoid becoming a victim by following these safety tips:

- Do not disclose any personal information over the phone such as your social security number and credit card number.
- Almost all thefts occur online, so be smart when doing your online banking. Always log off your account once finished.
- Do not download anything that pops up on your computer.
- Change your password regularly.
- Run an antivirus or security software all the time.
- Do not use online banking when on a Wi-Fi network at public places.
- Be Wiser When Handling Finances

You have probably learned your lesson the hard way. But what is important is that you learn from it and act on it. This way, you will not fall victim of this scrupulous scheme again and somehow learn how to play this tricky game.

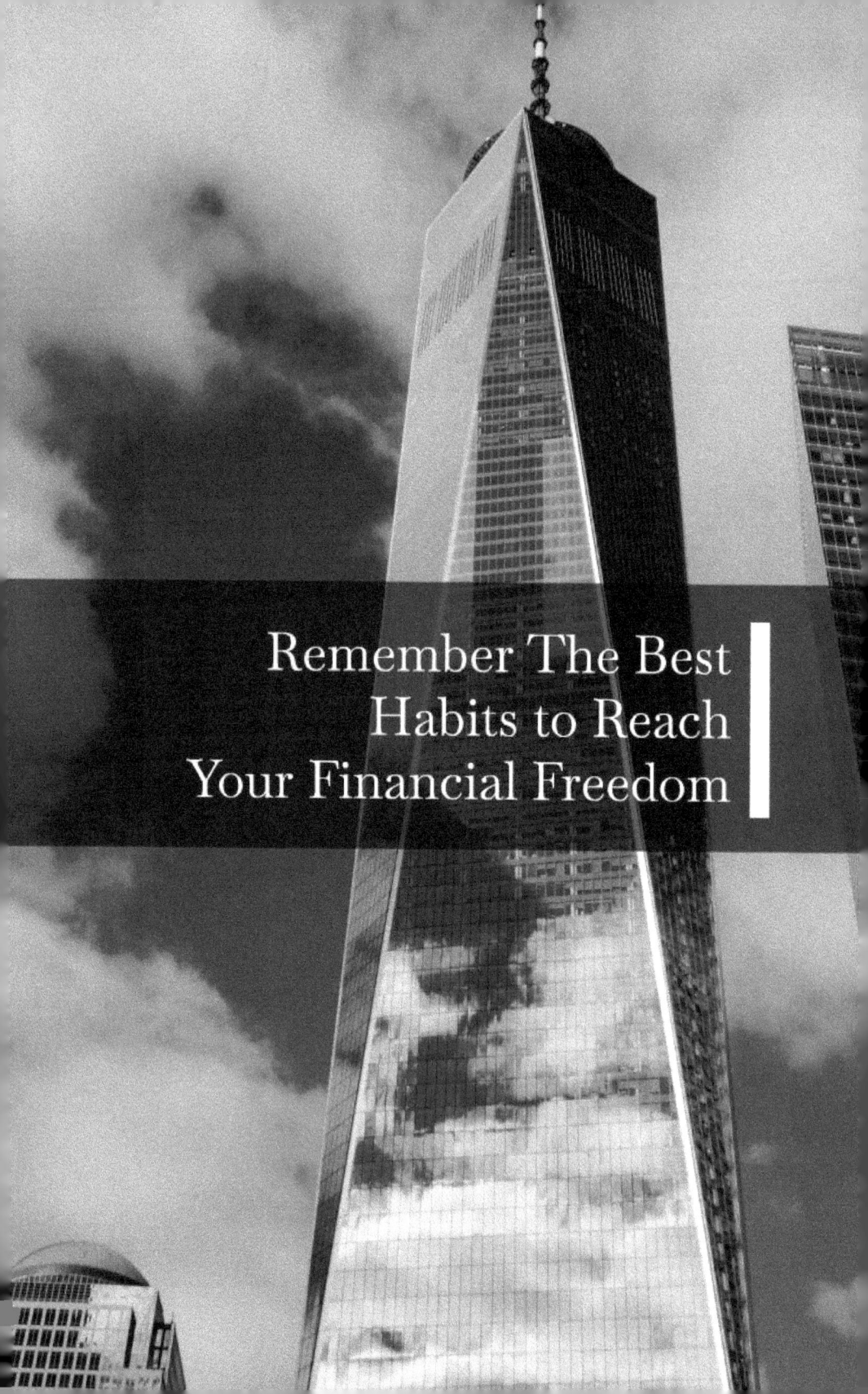

Remember The Best Habits to Reach Your Financial Freedom

Chapter 2.

Budgeting And Saving

Everyone needs to have a budget. By having a budget, you are able to track your income and expenditures. This is an effective measure to keep yourself in line and know your spending limits. It is also a good way to see how much money you have left after fulfilling your obligations. Another benefit of having a budget is that you have a hand in controlling spending unnecessarily on your credit card. You are able to use your credit card on small purchases that can be repaid quickly and boost your credit score.

Whatever spare money you have left can be put in a savings account to use as a down payment on a new car or that trip to Hawaii you have been dreaming about. In short, having money stashed away for a rainy day can help ease the burden should you encounter unforeseen circumstances. By squirreling away your money, you are less likely to max out your credit card because you are building up a little nest egg.

Benefits of Saving and Budgeting

There are many advantages and benefits to drawing up a budget and having a savings account. I am going to share a couple of these benefits with you to prove that it is possible to be financially responsible and independent. In the long run, your decision to budget accordingly and save will give you a sense of accomplishment.

Emergencies

Emergencies tend to pop up when least expected. When drawing up your monthly budget, you do not normally set aside money for emergencies. When a medical emergency presents itself, instead of maxing out your credit card or applying for a loan, you can make use of your savings. No matter the emergency, whether it is your car breaking or damage to your house, you do not budget for the unpredictable circumstances.

Retrenchment

Nothing can prepare you for losing your job. This is one event that can completely blindside you and everyone involved. This is also one that you can't foresee. Your savings will come in handy and soften the blow until you are able to find a new job or an alternative means of income.

Retirement

If you start saving from a young age and invest your money wisely, you will be able to retire comfortably. In my opinion, this is something that should be included in your monthly budget from the time you are able to save. As your money grows over the years, you will be able to enjoy your retirement.

Down Payment on a Car

This could be an exciting goal to look forward to. This can be added to your budget from a young age. You will be able to build up a tidy amount until you have enough to choose your first car. Imagine what you would like and work towards making that dream a reality.

In Summary

You have to admit that you are excited about spending time working on your monthly budget and savings now. You have seen the possibilities. While you are saving and budgeting accordingly, you are boosting your credit score.

Chapter 3.

The Importance of Investing

Why Investing Is Important at Any Age?

When it comes to investing, the earlier you start the better off you will be. I was sadly nearly out of my twenties before I began investing, but even if you are well beyond this age, investing still holds a lot of importance. Investing offers you the ability to grow your total amount of money through passively gaining interest over time. When the virtues of investing are spelled out, the argument to become involved is quite persuasive; however the issue is that in the moment many of us choose to use money to immediate effect instead of saving and investing.

To demonstrate the importance of investing versus using your immediate cash on hand, one must merely look to a famous thought experiment: the penny problem. If I were to offer you one million dollars today, or interest gained on a penny doubling every day for a month, which offer would you take? Without thinking too hard about the problem, many would take the more immediate money of one million dollars. If you were to go with option one, instead of taking the interest accruing option, you would end up with nearly four and a half million dollars less than if you had taken the second option.

While a penny doubling every day might not seem like a great way to accrue a lot of interest, the moment you begin to break down the problem and look at the numbers, you begin to see that is by far the more profitable option. The key is that the penny accrues interest exponentially, so that while at day two you may only have two cents, by day eight you have $1.28. By day twenty you still have not earned as much as the initial million dollars, with only $5,242.88 accruing, but by day thirty the entire pool will have grown to $5,368,709.12. There are two important lessons I want you to gain from this example: one, interest is not intuitive to humans, meaning it is hard to grasp how quickly money can grow unless we plan out the math and show the outcome. Two, the true cost of not receiving the million dollars up front was waiting thirty days to gain far more money. This is a key principle to investing, as what you will be trading to gain income quickly is merely the time that you are apart from your money. While you did not have one million dollars that you could use for thirty dollars, you ended up with far more money at the end of the month.

There are two last aspects of this example that are very important: what could you have done in those thirty days with one million dollars, and what is your tax obligation? In the penny example, it is doubtful that you could have quintupled your money within thirty days; however there are plenty of real world scenarios where you would have been able to earn more on the initial upfront cash versus leaving money in an interest bearing account. The million dollars as upfront cash could have been invested to gain interest much faster than the base amount if you had left it in the account. You must also consider what your tax liability is on either sum of money. Right now the disparity between the accounts is four and a half million dollars, where you earn much more by keeping a penny in the savings account. Suppose that the disparity was far less, something on the order of just $50,000. In this case, the million dollars upfront is far more tempting, as you are gaining marginally more compared to the original scenario presented. What this does not yield into account is the tax liability on the cash gained immediately versus what you would have earned within thirty days. In general the faster that you realize profit from an investment, the more costly the tax liability. The longer you wait, the lower the tax liability. This means that you might gain far more than 50k if you held onto the investment for thirty days, not because the sum of money is much larger to begin with, but because the tax rate is far more favorable. This is a microcosm example, and for short difference in time of only thirty days, the actual tax liability is likely to be the same, but for longer stretches of time there are stark differences.

Compound Interest

You should know quite well that if someone offers you a deal to double a penny for thirty days you should certainly take it, but in the real world investing is much more difficult. You will not find these incredible opportunities so easily. However the penny example demonstrates an important aspect of investing, and one that makes it possible for your money to earn interest faster, compound interest. Compound interest allows for interest to be gained on interest that you have already accrued. The definition might seem complicated, but the concept is quite simple. In the penny example above, you can see how compound interest works, although in unrealistic scenario. The interest that is gained on the penny is doubled every day, and the new sum is the one that is doubling, allowing for the money to grow at such an exponential rate. In real terms, we have to look to a much tamer example.

Imagine that you had one hundred dollars appreciating at one percent interest, and this this is compounded four times a year. You would assume that the interest you would earn at the end of one year to be one dollar, or just one percent of your base investment, but this is not entirely accurate. It is compounding, and being added at four times per year, so after three months you have earned $0.25, or one quarter of that one percent interest. What's of note is that this small sum is added back into the base investment so that when the next interest period comes about, another three months, you are earning interest on $100.25 and not just $100. At the end of the initial year this has essentially happened four times. After quarter one, you have earned $100.25, quarter two $100.50, quarter three $100.76, and quarter four $101.02. These numbers are not far off the one percent interest that you may have been originally expecting, but you can see that since the interest is compounding, you are on earning more just one quarter of one percent. Since the interest is being counted in the new sum, you are earning interest at a much faster rate. In this example, with very modest numbers, this only equals a difference of two cents, but with larger sums of money, and greater interest rates, this number can grow very quickly.

In addition, there is a separate idea of compound interest, and that is taking the interest from one investment and carrying it over to another. This is not as institutionalized as compound interest once per quarter, and is left up to the individual to work out the details. You can see though that if you were to keep track of all of the interest that you accumulated, and moved this interest to different investment ventures, your interest would grow at an accelerated rate. It is this idea of compound interest, and always using the interest gained from old investments to carry over to new interest that you can also start to see the importance of starting to invest as soon as you can. The longer you invest, regardless of the total quantity of your investments, the better off you will be. The principle of interest accruing on top of interest is simply too powerful to ignore.

Why You Have to Invest, Even When It Is a Financial Strain

Compound interest should be a fairly compelling argument for why it is to your advantage to start saving as soon as possible, however I know how difficult investing can seem when you are under financial strain. Just a few years ago I would have had difficulty making any sort of investments in my future. I was working a moderately paying job in a very expensive city; between rent, food and travel I was consuming so much of my paycheck that investing didn't seem worth the time. This is a common mentality, and one that I understand, but it is also a mentality that will hurt you. You must start saving and investing as soon as you can, as even miniscule amounts of your salary invested will equal big gains in the long run.

Chapter 4.

How To Ensure Customers Fall In love With Your Business

A substantial factor in your business's long-term success is not just attracting however likewise pleasing and retaining consumers. As a small business owner, you may be on the front lines of dealing with your organization's consumers.

However, if you have workers, they'll likely be handling clients, too. Therefore, the importance of offering exceptional client service need to be clear to everyone in your organization who has any effect (direct or indirect) on customer satisfaction. This includes the receptionist, the accounts receivable clerk, the shipment truck chauffeur, and lots of others. Although the level of customer care in lots of organizations leaves much to be preferred, just a silly company owner would assume that dissatisfied consumers will continue to tolerate poor service or purchase products that don't perform.

Customers usually have many options, so if you and your employees don't please your clients' requirements, you'll likely deal with these unpleasant.

Now more than ever, clients have lots of choices for buying what your company has to provide. For the vast bulk of businesses, competition is intense at the global, national, state, local, and regional levels. It's only a matter of time prior to your unhappyn customers become your competitors' newest consumers. Negative word-of-mouth: Even even worse than losing dissatisfied customers to the competition is negative word-of-mouth where unhappy consumers talk and tell other customers, why they would not buy your product or services.

Your competitors are more than pleased to recount the unfavorable stories they've heard from your irritated customers. All this talk will definitely tarnish your business's track record.

Maintaining Your Customer Base.

As the owner of a small organization, you require to keep your consumers pleased. How? Well, you have a huge effect on your customers' satisfaction through your company's items and services and the method in which you provide them. This area offers you with the secrets to keeping your customers pleased. Of course, not all consumers will stay loyal and pleased to your service. We likewise discuss how you can find out from customer defections to lessen their occurring in the future.

Getting it right the very first time.

As a small-business owner, if you don't get your item or service right the very first time, you might not have a second possibility with consumers. Clients aren't foolish, and if you offer them inferior merchandise-- particularly when better product is offered from other sources-- they will not return the next time they're in the market for the product or services you use. What's more, they'll inform others of their lousy experience with your business.

Large companies generally have adequate cash reserves developed to weather a storm, but the typical small-business owner does not.

All businesses have services or products to offer often businesses get too concentrated on those product or services, providing brief shrift to the accompanying client service that customers. Expect. Perhaps you can't readily define the term customer care.

Let's turn the tables now. What sort of experience do your customers have when they do business with your company? Are your workers well trained and experienced? Do they pride themselves in providing excellent customer care? Do you make it easy for your clients to do company with you? You can never be too excellent at customer care and undoubtedly there's always room for enhancement.

Principles for delivering fantastic Customer Service

Put your clients first.
This means doing everything in your power to fulfill their requirements and seeing things from the customer's viewpoint. Do things for their benefit and make certain your treatments are effective.

Always acknowledge clients. In face to face interactions a smile, eye contact or a nod in the consumer's instructions can make all the difference. No-one likes being disregarded or made to feel they are wearing an invisibility cloak.

Make your routine consumers feel valued. It's much simpler to win service from existing consumers than it is to discover new clients. If you have a great memory for people and the things that matter to them, it assists. If you don't, you can constantly make a couple of baby crib notes in your consumer files.

Constantly listen to your clients.
High quality listening is one of the most crucial things you can do for your customers.

Treat customers with respect at all times. If the customers themselves are less than respectful or well behaved, common courtesies should never be neglected no matter how hectic your personnel are or undoubtedly. Likewise, it is essential to respect individuals whatever their background or lifestyle.

There are no doubt consumers can be demanding and at times downright unreasonable. It's likewise reasonable to say that no-one ever won an argument with a customer.

Be willing to 'go above and beyond' for your clients. Often it's the small things that can make a substantial distinction, doing something the consumer did not expect. At other times it may indicate taking out all the stops to deal with an issue.

Clients can be unpredictable and there's no space for complacency in providing consumer service. If you desire to remain ahead of the competition then it's essential to gather feedback from your consumers about your items or services.

Make things easy for your consumers. Whether you handle clients generally online, over the telephone or face to deal with, it should be easy for them to do service with you. Do not anticipate them to leap through unnecessary hoops or to be kept waiting.

Show appreciation for your customers. If you didn't have customers, remember your service wouldn't exist. Make a point of thanking your clients for working with you. Be genuine in what you state. Clients will translucent incorrect declarations or beliefs and they will not be impressed.

Chapter 5.

What Is Credit Counseling?

At times, an individual might be faced with critical financial instability, especially when his debts are out of control. Faced with such a menace, it is advisable to take time and think of the right solution to the situation. One can even seek for advice in order to reach a decision that will not cost him. The possible remedies in the market include visiting credit counselors and debt-consolidators. Both methods are common in that they will help you to contain the situation. Nevertheless, you need to weigh both options to ensure that you choose the right one depending on the weight of your financial situation.

Credit counselors, these are professionals who will assist you to untangle your financial woes on daily basis. Individuals running these counseling firms have deep knowledge in debt management and other options that can be applied to minimize debts. Credit counselors provide several alternatives, after which the borrower can manage his debts afterwards.

With the help of the expert, the borrower prepares a realistic budget. This budget stresses mainly on how the borrower spends his money. By the time the counseling process is over, the borrower will come into terms with what exactly caused the debt. The Credit counselors will help the borrower to diagnose the cause so that he will not repeat the same mistake once again. The budget created eliminates any unnecessary expenditure as well as setting tough look at the spending habits of the borrower.

The Credit counselors afterwards supply the borrower with possible options to eliminate all the financial obligations facing him or her. Some of the possible options are learning on debt management, debt consolidation, personal bankruptcy and enlightenment on how to settle ones debt. Basically, the choice of these options will be catalyzed by the severity of debt facing the borrower.

Generally, credit counselors will only enlighten a borrower on how to contain any debt menace on their own. These methods are effective when one is not faced by fatal punishments such as loosing possession of his assets. In such situations, it is advisable to visit debt-consolidators.

Debt-consolidator, although common with credit counselors in that they help borrower contain debt menace, they specifically save borrowers from losing their property or from running bankrupt. Plans given by Debt-consolidator will give a borrower financial freedom within a short period.

Debt-consolidators will require the borrower to have good credit rating in order to qualify for their plans. If one qualifies for the consolidation plans, Debt-consolidators will extend consolidation loans to them. Basically, these are loans inclusive of all the current balances the borrower has not been able to meet. The consolidation of loans relieves the borrower from any current debt obligation, hence good for someone close to losing his personal assets to an unpaid lender.

For a borrower to make the right choice, he needs to weigh to benefits and limitations of each option. For example, debt management might affect future reputation in that lenders might be reluctant in giving the borrower loan as he is presumed to be irresponsible; debt settlement might not be effective in clearing the whole portion of the loan amount hence impairing the borrower's credit rating while the price of debt consolidation is an increased debt for settlement of the current debt.

When it's Time to Seek Counseling

So how exactly do you know when it's time to seek out help? Well essentially there are 3 stages of recovery that you should think about. Stage 1 is self-help. Your credit card and other debts are in such a way that you can essentially take care of it yourself through using credit elimination tactics and making small, logical decisions on how to save money and pay off debts. Stage 2 is when your debts become unmanageable and you decide you need outside help; that's where credit counseling agencies come into play. Stage 3 is when even your outside help doesn't know what to do and your only logical recourse is to file for bankruptcy.

It is probably time to go to credit counseling if you can't control your debt. If you can't make your payments or you know you can't pay off your debt without help, you need this type of counseling. Don't be afraid to answer your phone because it may be collectors calling. Don't struggle to pay all your bills. Don't accept that you will be in debt the rest of your life. Go to credit counseling.

Going to this type of counseling is better than living in fear, in debt, or filing for bankruptcy. Credit counselors may be able to negotiate with credit card companies and get interest lowered or late fees forgiven. It is not guaranteed, but you can certainly try to find a counselor that can do so. A credit counselor will also help you figure out a budget after they look at how much you make, how much your debt is, and how much your utility bills are. Following a counselor's advice and sticking to a budget is really important when trying to get out of debt. It may be difficult, but you will have an amazing feeling when you have no more debt.

Credit counselors are not there to judge you; it is their job to help you. Get counseling recommendations from your bank, credit card companies, or a friend. Make sure a credit counselor is certified. You want a professional that knows exactly what they are doing.

Seeking credit counseling is a huge step to recovering from debt. It is the right thing to do if you have gotten in way over your head. Living in debt is not fun and credit counseling can help you.

That being said, if your debt is actually manageable then you could just be wasting a lot of money by hiring a debt settlement or debt counseling company. In the long run it could save you a lot of money.

Chapter 6.

Right Mindset for Credit Management

Financial problems can be and usually are overwhelming. To make these situations worse, most people do not even know where to begin to solve these financial dilemmas. Basic consumer debt will chain you into slavery and you could possibly spend your life held down by your own obligations to repay these loans.

The person or institution lending you the money is trusting that you have the ability to hold up your end of the bargain, basically.

What type of credit should you get? That depends on what you plan to do with the money. The most used types of credit are secured and signature credits. For smaller loans, there's no need for that, as no institution would like to end up with a store of household items, so they lend you money or issue a credit card in your name simply based on the strength of your credit so far.

You can take advantage of budgeting and other techniques, such as debt consolidation, debt settlement, credit counseling, and bankruptcy procedures. You just have to choose the best strategy that will work for you.

When choosing from the various options, you have to consider your debt level, your discipline, and plans for the future.

7 Tips to Manage Your Credit

Using consolidation or settlement strategies to pay down debts
Debt consolidation is another strategy that can be used to manage your debts. It involves combining two or more debts at a lower interest rate than you are currently at.

But it is worth doing your research and making some phone calls to see if there is a company that is willing to work with you. If you can lower your monthly bill to a manageable level, at an interest rate that is reasonable, that can make all the difference in handling your debt.

It is just that consolidation and settlement options rose in popularity during the recent financial crisis making it appear in more articles and news pieces than ever before.

Negotiate with Credit Companies
Another thing not a lot of people know is that you can negotiate with credit companies. So you are able to take the collection letter they send you or a past due notice that has been sent to you and discuss it with them. In many cases they will take a lower amount than what is on the bill just so that they can guarantee they will get something

If you talk to the collection agency and they agree to take a lesser amount you will have to send that payment in full. Make sure that when you send them the check you write out the words 'paid in full' on the check. Make a copy of the check for your own records as well. Once they cash that check your account is legally considered to be paid in full and they are no longer able to come after you for more money.

Cut the Credit Cards

Choose a card that will work anywhere such as a major credit card company.

The best thing to do is make one to two small purchases on your credit card every few months. Try to space out using different cards so that none of them get taken but you do not owe very much money each month.

Talking to Creditors

Tell them the reason why you are having a difficult time paying the debts. Most companies will negotiate a modified payment plan so monthly payments become more manageable. If you wait for the accounts to go into default, it can and most likely will affect your credit score negatively, which is what we are looking to avoid. Once in default, the collector will start calling.

Credit Counseling

Credit counseling is a service offered by some organizations to borrowers seeking advice on how they can manage their finances. It usually includes budgeting, workshops, and educational resources. A counselor must receive training and certification in budgeting, money and debt management, and consumer credit.

Debt Management Plan

The credit counselor negotiates with the creditors and drafts a payment schedule. Creditors may be amenable to waive some fees or reduce interest rates. Usually, a debt management plan takes about 4 years to be completed, depending on your amount of debt.

This is a great option for someone who would like to be "hands off" while repaying their debt and repairing their credit.

Debt Settlement Program

A debt settlement program can be risky, so you have to consider some factors before taking advantage of it. Many of these programs require that you deposit money on an account for at least 3 years before the debt settlement company can settle your debts.

Another aspect to consider is that some creditors will not negotiate for a debt settlement; therefore, the debt settlement company may not be able to pay some of your debts. In addition, some of these debt settlement companies pay off smaller debts first, leaving the large debts to continue growing.

The debt settlement company will suggest that you stop paying your creditors. This decision will result in a significant drop to your credit score. The debts will also incur fees and penalties for nonpayment. A debt settlement program is only as good as the debt settlement company that offers it.

Conclusion

Thank you for making it to the end. So far in this wonderful exposition, I have unveiled the core truths about credit and creditworthiness and we have discussed the most vital strategies by which you can repair your credit and boost your credit score from bad to excellent all by yourself. However, it is important not to get so carried away in your desperation to repair your credit that you begin to indulge in the most common errors which may ultimately sabotage your efforts. As a takeaway package, I present to you some of the most salient mistakes to watch against as you repair your credit. From my encounter with people in your shoes who have one difficulty or the other with their credit history, these mistakes are both common and subtle. As a matter of fact, some of them seem to be solutions or hacks in credit repair but they ultimately undo your efforts. Get your highlighter ready!

The Most Salient Mistakes to Avoid

Failure to Check Credit Reports

This is perhaps the most foundational problem in credit repair. It stems from stark ignorance or mere recklessness or a poor finance-related habit or the intentional refusal to face the facts of your credit status. Well, the truth is that the refusal to own up to your credit mess doesn't take it away. The reality will come haunting you the moment you step into a bank to request loan or you need to apply for a new job and the employer requests it! Regularly checking your credit report keeps you updated with your credit status and helps you identify problem areas to thrash out. It also keeps you abreast with the specific areas where your report is being negatively affected, what information to address or dispute, and what part of your financial involvements to focus on. As far as credit is concerned, the more you know the better for your credit status. Mores so, bear in mind that it is a great disservice to yourself to wait till a financial firm or employer requests your credit reports before you check them up yourself. There are several known online platforms to check your reports. A typical example is the Federal Trade Commission Free Credits Report page.

Failure to Pay Down Debt Quickly

What many do not realize is that paying off your debts, and quickly too, is one of the most assured ways to remedy your bad credit. The way out is to offset your debts in small regular bits. Staying true to a particular pattern of debt clearance greatly improves your credit score. Take down credits seriously, especially the credit cards that are close to being maxed out. Another similarly significant approach is to pay your installment loans such as student loans and auto loans, depending on which ones apply to you. Constantly reducing your loans and debts does not only improve your credit score but sells you as a dependable and responsible client to future employers, loan firms, banks and other finance-related organizations.

Improper or No Documentation

Documentation is highly essential to arriving at an awesome credit score. It is wrong to fail to take documentation of every financial activity you engage in. Your spending history is one of the factors put into consideration by credit bureaus to calculate your credit score. This explains why you should never agree to an oral agreement; however flimsy it seems. All payments should be backed with paperwork or at least receipts. In as much as there is a financial commitment attached to it, ensure you have it properly documented. Your documented payments and financial activities come in handy when or if you have a reason to dispute a report later in the future. Bureaus do not work with oral agreements, so if you have been offsetting a debt or repaying a loan, for example, ensure it is well documented.

Canceling Credit Card Accounts

Is this really a good idea? Maybe not! You can never increase your credit score by closing your credit cards. The truth about your credit report, as you have learned so far, is that there are so many factors in place. Closing a credit card account with many bad records such as debts, late payments, and so on, seems to be able to boost your credit score, but on the contrary, that is not so. This is because the length of your credit history is one of the major factors that input your credit report. Closing an account does nothing but to reduce the length of your credit card history, thereby making you lose some points in that regard. The most vital way out is to keep the accounts and reduce the low payments on them.

I hope you have learned something

Dave R W Graham

Other Author's Works

Stock Market Investing for Beginners and Options Trading Crash Course:

Master Like an Intelligent Investor the Stocks, ETFs, Bonds, Futures, Forex Markets. Leverage Your Capital with Options Trading.

Swing and Day Trading Strategies:

A Crash Course To Learn Technical Analysis, Money Management, Discipline Building Your Perfect Strategies for Day Trade For A Living and Generate Your Passive Income.

Investing and Trading Strategies:

4 books in 1: The Complete Crash Course with Proven Strategies to Become a Profitable Trader in the Financial Markets and Stop Living Paycheck to Paycheck.

Author's Note

Thanks for reading my book. If you want to learn more about personal finance, investments, trading, and business, I suggest you follow my author page on Amazon. Through my books, I have decided to share with you the know-how that has allowed me to achieve my financial freedom, to accumulate wealth, and to live the life I want with my family.

My goal is to show you the path with useful and applicable information for reaching your targets. Only you will be able to tread that path as I did… and now, I'm sharing what I know.

To your wealth!

Dave R. W. Graham

©Copyright 2020 by Dave Robert Warren Graham

– All rights reserved –

CPSIA information can be obtained
at www.ICGtesting.com
Printed in the USA
LVHW010558060221
678443LV00014B/929